The Plight of English

THE PLIGHT OF ENGLISH

Ambiguities, Cacophonies and Other Violations of Our Language

Basil Cottle
MA (Wales), PhD (Bristol)
Senior Lecturer in English, University of Bristol

RLINGTON HOUSE·PUBLISHERS
NEW ROCHELLE, N. Y.

Library of Congress Cataloging in Publication Data

Cottle, Basil.
  The Plight of English.

  Includes index.
  1. English language. I. Title.
PE1072.C58   428'.009'047   74–26996
ISBN 0–87000–307–0

CONTENTS

To
Dennis Cutter
of
Longwell Green
Bristol

I

THE PRESENT STATE OF
THE LANGUAGE

The publishers had invited me to write this book, and I confided in a colleague. His comment was frank and grave: 'You could damn yourself by writing a book like that.' He meant, of course, that if I set myself up as a prescriptive grammarian or stylist, my readers would be on the alert for every lapse or pedantry, every archaism or modern vulgarism, every ignoble mark of my insular love of our language; yet when he had left me, I reflected on his statement and cheerfully realised that it could be interpreted in thirty-six different ways. 'You' is either *you*, *B. Cottle* or *one* (as in 'You need oxygen on top of Everest', a scene in which my presence would be inappropriate); 'could' is either *were able to* (the past tense of *can*) or a future tense denoting both risk ('You could blow yourself up') and opportunity ('You could win the prize'); 'damn' has at least three clear senses—*condemn, curse,* or *dispatch to hell* (and, indeed, the speaker belonged to a sect which has an official belief in this arrangement); 'like that' is either (a book) *of that nature* or (writing) *in that manner*. Formally, therefore, the possible interpretations are $2 \times 3 \times 3 \times 2 = 36$; and though most of these would occur only to a fool, the pitfalls of such a sentence, spoken though it was by a highly educated and articulate person, at once seemed to me sufficient justification for the dismayed and earnest examination, now to follow, of the present state of English.

My count of thirty-six was, in fact, modest, and relates only to the sentence in static print; if we add the variations made available by the rise and fall of the speaking voice, we shall find further regrettable riches of meaning. '*You*' stressed can imply 'You're welcome to that—*I* wouldn't touch it'; '*could*', the barest possibility; '*yourself*', the biter bit, the critic caught in his own trap and his victims at liberty; merely '*writing*', the least risky part of the procedure, whereas publishing (say) would be even more disastrous; 'a *book*', the danger of going beyond a brief article or pamphlet. A mathematician assures me that we have now reached 576 feasible interpretations; even if we ignore those induced by intonation and by a pliant tongue, it is still certain that we are dealing with a language which has got itself into at least one kind of mess—the tangle of ambiguity and imprecision. But English has been praised for being so plain, expressive, and direct; are these lost or vanishing virtues, can they even now be retrieved, is their decay part of an inevitable linguistic process, and was the earlier state of the language so very much better? Am I, indeed, being fussy?—finding confusion where only a fool would be confused, diagnosing decay where there is rude health, and nostalgically looking back to a form of language equally but differently plagued?

Now some of the problems of our sorely tried sentence are predominantly semantic. The word *damn* has retained or acquired multiple meanings—theological, legal, and

8

personal; beyond the possible bounds of the sentence, it is likely that for many speakers it also carries an overtone as having been their first juvenile swearword, the mildest of such. Somerset Maugham, in *The Circle*, lets a fastidious character rebuke his wife for saying 'Damn!', whereat she produces the argument 'If you're not going to say damn when a thing's damnable, when are you going to say it?'; and little girls in the 1890s thought it deliciously depraved to parody Dekker with 'Golden slumbers damn your eyes'. Obviously, a word to use with caution; quite apart from its threefold 'meaning' which I isolated earlier, it has other dimensions, and the reader or listener will be further bemused and inhibited by it.

But another source of confusion is grammatical, and not a matter of shifts in 'meaning': the meagre grammatical machinery whereby our nouns, adjectives, verbs, and adverbs are inflected. I must not suggest, of course, that grammatical inflexions are not meaningful, but making a noun plural by adding *s* is not as radical intellectually as distinguishing the yellow flag, peril, and press. We now use fewer inflexions than formerly—many fewer, for instance, than did Chaucer 600 years ago; Welsh, French, and German use many more, and Classical Greek had a magnificent array which contributed to (though it could not wholly cause) the great expressiveness of that language. Yet inflexions are not a prerequisite of a language, and a case against their paucity in English would have to be closely argued and might be incapable of proof. The idiom of today can be sustained largely by the stems of operative words (the 'nominative singular' and the 'infinitive'—to use a terminology which I wish I could avoid) linked by little prepositions or conjunctions, though there is no way of avoiding a trail of -(e)s, -(e)n, -ed (and other dentals), -er, -est, -ing, and -ly. The admired simplicity of feeling in

> Go to Joan Glover
> And tell her I love her

is matched by an apparent simplicity of grammar (though this reliance on monosyllables has in it the seeds of a less admirable complexity); the one concession to historical grammar is the dative and accusative *her* where the nominative *she* would give the same 'meaning', but Bristolians add their own refinement to this, cheerfully switching the cases with such a statement as ' 'Er wouldn't suit I'—an idiom which general opinion thinks unhandy. Fossilised, too, in Miss Glover's surname is the -er suffix which we retain in many 'doer' or 'maker' nouns, but which we cannot automatically apply when we feel like it; we can no longer assume that 'shirter' or 'socker' will be satisfactory words, and even 'glover', as a vocabulary element and not as a surname, is probably moribund or dead in areas away from such glovemaking centres as Yeovil.

Our original sentence comes to little harm in the shallows of its grammar; 'could' is (despite the various meanings offered) the past tense of 'can', though very ill spelt with its parasitic -l- borrowed from 'would' and 'should'; 'writing' bears an inflexion still vigorous (too vigorous, indeed, for it has adopted two different functions and forms two parts of speech); and only 'like that' would be focused by an inflexion, to prove it either an adjective phrase in the accusative case or an adverb phrase. But when a sentence is longer, and decked with phrases and clauses, or when—as often in verse—the words are not in a pertinent order, we may feel the lack of precise grammatical relationships. It is easy to be lulled by the nobility of Collins's

> How sleep the Brave who sink to rest
> By all their Country's wishes blest!
> When Spring, with dewy fingers cold . . .

But to what does 'blest' refer, the Brave or their rest?—a problem soluble only by marking it clearly as a nominative plural or as a dative (or something similar—let us call it 'prepositional') singular agreeing with 'rest' after a preposition. Are they (or their rest) blest by the wishes of all their Country ('all' being genitive singular in agreement with 'Country's') or by all the wishes of their Country ('all' being prepositional plural in agreement with 'wishes')? Is 'rest' perhaps not a noun at all, but a verb in the infinitive ('so as to rest')? Are Spring's dewy fingers 'cold' (prepositional plural after 'with'), or is she 'cold' (nominative singular) with having dewy fingers? It will be agreed that I am not looking for trouble here, or wantonly finding fault; I am using a serious and well loved poem to show that a lightly inflected language such as English cannot safely disarray its word-order, however poetical it may seem to do so.

A friend of mine has regretted aloud our 'silent grammatical machinery' and has longed for more 'grinding of grammatical gears'. At first it seems easy to refute him: we don't need an elaborate inflexional system, our compensation for it being prepositions (instead of case-endings), auxiliary verbs (instead of endings to mark tense, mood, and voice), and nominative pronouns (to

11

obviate verb-endings for person and number). Ideally, this is a pretty complete answer; but the reality shows only a half-hearted escape from synthesis into analysis, and an apparent emancipation which only presents new problems of imprecision and cacophony. Thus no dissociated particle has been devised to make nouns plural, and we still cling to the genitive singular in -'*s* (but only with animates, for no perfect reason) and the absurd genitive plural in -*s*'; I shall be writing harshly about this ubiquitous *s*. We also pretend to have a dative noun, when we 'give the boy the book'; but we cannot 'give the book the boy', and it is clear that the dead body of this 'case' revives only when the word-order allows it. As for auxiliary verbs, there will be a sombre tale to tell here soon of their slow erosion and of their present ruin; in the form they exist in, they are not worth having. Our nominative pronouns *do* adequately cover the niceties of verb-endings for first, second, and third persons singular and plural (though the singular *you* is a makeshift); so that it is strange that the third person singular present indicative still clings to privilege and keeps an -*s*, another monotonous -*s*.

Thus our compensation for a full inflexional system is now incomplete and dangerous; it can also be very ugly. Someone has said, not aptly, that English is 'degenerating into monosyllabification', and it is certain that our sentences can easily sound like a stick being drawn along railings; we could condone our clusters of little prepositions if they firmly surrounded and placed their nouns in an indisputable context, but they have multiple meanings, and when used irresponsibly they jam the traffic of their sentences. 'For me, for example, for years the question has been as to whether in the event of . . .' is the kind of rambling that constitutes the real menace of the preposition—not whether it is used to end a sentence with. Phrases such as 'in the light of' may sound judicious, but will often be temporising and futile, or mixed in their metaphors, whereas insistence that etymologically a preposition should be 'placed before' is as useful as saying that the lady who is 'the cynosure of all eyes' at the ball is etymologically the dog's tail.

I am sure that the greatest peril for our language is a growing imprecision, which ranges from a fine shade of misinterpretation to downright misunderstanding; its diagnosis and treatment ought to form the staple of this book. Cacophony comes second, and is regrettable, but it matters far less. The third tender spot is Style and Taste (we had better dignify them with capital letters); but we are told that these are a wholly subjective affair, so is it right for me to dogmatise or even to plead? Well, fortunately, this is a wholly subjective book, written mainly with eye, ear, and heart; it is meant to belong to no 'school', it prefers passion and commonsense (at least, my version of this) to linguistic theory, and the authorities whom it quotes are mainly the current users and misusers of our language. Despite my own principal interest in the older period of English, I shall try here to consider our language as it is; its splendour is still real, and often an enhancement of what went before; its meanness is sometimes historically based, sometimes perverse. But I do not want to see these features as *comparatively* good or bad; nothing in our linguistic history need take the credit for present genius or the blame for present slovenliness. Similarly, it seems to me that comparison with other languages is pointless in the context of this book; their richer inflexional system may give us wistful ideas, the alphabets of Welsh or Spanish or Albanian may make us rationally jealous, some may madly hanker after a return to grammatical gender or an extension of our verb system to include the Russian 'aspects', and a programmed maoist may even advocate the Chinese way of going about language; but English remains very serviceable, and pruned of its grosser faults it would have the highest claim to be the ideal universal tongue.

THE PRODIGAL VOCABULARY

We have by far the largest vocabulary of any language.
The great thirteen-volume *Oxford English Dictionary* occu-
pies over 16,000 huge columned pages, contains over
414,000 words, and has single words for a wheeled step-
ladder to service the inner aisle roofs of York Minster, for
a printers' annual beanfeast or picnic, and for the faculty
of making pleasant discoveries by accident; lest I inflict
suspense, I must quickly add that these are *fleet*, *wayzgoose*,
and *serendipity*, and that there are many more just as
strange in their luxurious exactness. All these riches
derive partly from the genius and imagination of speakers
and writers, partly from the enlarged horizons in Britain's
days of acquiring an empire, and largely from the well
known layering of our vocabulary in three great language
stocks—Germanic (in its Old English form, with some
Norse) before 1066, Romance (Norman and, later, Cen-
tral French) thereafter, and Classical with increasing emphasis during and after the Renaissance. Medical men, it
would seem, could hardly get along without this last great
layer of Latin and, especially, Greek; yet had we early
called the process of appendicectomy 'hanger-on-cutting-
out', or based our words for gingivitis and the Trinity on

good old Germanic methods and called them 'tooth-flesh-smart' and 'Threefoldhood', we might pardonably wonder whether the alien words were needed. In the last century William Barnes, valiantly eternising the Dorset dialect, expressed *his* wonder in his coining of words such as *folkwain*, for an omnibus; he was too late, of course, and even those who were ignorant of the origin of *omnibus* (as was the MP who made the plural *omnibi*) or who regretted its existence ('What is it that roareth thus?/Can it be the motor bus?') helped to fix a form which has settled happily into the vocabulary as *bus* or (in careful hands) *'bus*. I shall later have a lot to say about the many compound nouns that have been luckier than *folkwain*; few of them would now seem as bizarre as the *New Statesman* competitor's suggestion *upgangflow* for an escalator, but who knows what the fate of *escalator* will be now that it is assailed by the absurd escalation of the verb *to escalate*?

There is no Academy, no higher power, to give or withhold authority for new words; and this licence has not in general been abused. From Shakespeare's time onward there has been inventiveness and adaptation, to the great enrichment of the language; and our own century, with impudent and ranging wit, has formed dashing but ephemeral words that are packed with allusion: Ogden Nash's *polterguest* is useful for the visitor who can't be fended off the washing-up, and a *New Statesman* competitor saw secondary modern schoolchildren *gadarening* home. For the purposes of advertisement, an expensively fed cat is an *aristocat*, and a kettle that turns itself off is a *forgettle*—this is the merest trick, but has the merits of a ridiculous humour that reconciles the unlike. When, however, the writer has strained to say something new, and has pretended that to describe the sea as *snot-green* is anything more than compressing a rather nasty simile, the achievement is slighter.

The grammatical framework of English is such that we can fit into it any useful word from abroad. It would be a great nuisance if *lassoo* had had to be pressed into a second declension noun in *-us* and a first conjugation verb in *-o*, as in a language of Latin type; instead, *-s* is cobbled on when necessary, and the word is acclimatised. Again, though we have many lovely words, not always tied to lovely things (*cellar-door* being a charming example), we show no reluctance in adopting the awkward ones that bristle with consonants; we leave the gardener his eschscholtzia, the pharaoh his pschent. Indeed, our vocabulary has words of every shape and aspect, and of every sound and allusion, so that it is easy and unsubtle to create the kind of onomatopoeia whereby Tennyson lets the bare black cliff clang round Bedivere before his sudden arrival at the level lake and the long glories of the winter moon; Masefield did this notoriously well in *Cargoes*, where the three stanzas depict and set to music the centuried and sultry, the opulent, and the downright grubby.

So far, in this chapter, there is little to disparage. The saturation of English with foreign words in the sixteenth and seventeenth centuries no doubt gave us some trivialities which would not now be missed, but a universal language has to deal in the coinage of its friends and rivals, and it would be mere jingoism now to trust only an eating-house and to avoid anything calling itself hotel, restaurant, or café; but the reassuring teashop is half-native, and the rougher classes always cut a café down to size by their hideous pronunciations *caff* and *cayf*. Whole departments of our lives are best covered by Latinate words, sometimes modified in their passage through French but often surprisingly unchanged from those universal forms that give them a useful currency among those who have been taught the Classics—who, alas, are growing fewer. Again, it is often quite false to speak of English and French 'synonyms' in our language; even setting aside subtler concepts, and using a pair quite simple to understand, we cannot claim absolute equivalence for *bloom* (from Old Norse) and *flower*. Very oddly, the swanky and pretentious word is not now the French one: 'Oh, what lovely blooms!'; King Alfred was 'England's bloom', whereas 'the flower of England' suggests a young generation; an irritating alternative spelling, *flour*, now means something different; the slang use of the participle of the cognate verb, *bloomin'*, adds a new dimension and may in time spoil the noun; to most people, *flower* probably means the whole plant, leaves and all, whereas *bloom* is the colourful top; a homonym *bloom* is from Old English, not Old Norse, and is a technical term from ironworking; Mrs Amelia Jenks Bloomer's invention may by now have conspired with *bloomin'* against the monosyllable. And so on, for hundreds of 'synonyms'.

There may be no discernible difference in 'meaning' between a building and an edifice, but those sensitive to the niceties of *gown* and *dress* and *frock* could extend their care to all other topics, which may be likewise affected by fashion and context and occasion and the company one is in. The apparent riches of our vocabulary may well be real; not only are most of the so-called synonyms delightfully and subtly distinguishable, but many apparently straightforward words are found on examination to have developed extra shades or flavours or tones or textures or,

I suppose, aromas. A word that reached us long ago, with one meaning only, may by now have lost that meaning totally or largely, though at the same time extending its application literally or figuratively, becoming more general or more precise, or occupying the position of some word now extinct. One of the oddest, and yet simplest, is *fair*, which in Middle English meant 'beautiful' or 'handsome', but now means variously 'blond/equitable/mediocre' and still (in *fair weather*) sort-of 'beautiful'; this is a silly state of affairs, and a warning that perhaps all is not well with our great cornucopia of words. Is our vocabulary nobly rich, or is it bloated?

Let me say at once that I am not presuming to *blame* our language or its users for what has happened to many of our words. Remarks such as 'a static language is a dead language' are rife, though there is perhaps no adequate excuse for what has happened to *fair*. But people who accept such an adage should never use archaisms for fun; this contributes to the confusion, and is a conversational method barren of wit. Instead of saying 'I'll see thee anon', reflect that *anon* really meant (when it was current) 'at once'; hesitate to use 'fair lady', now that it has been seen how utterly equivocal it is; be careful of 'come Michaelmas' if you don't quite know what it implies; and don't follow Coleridge into using 'eftsoons': you have words enough, without pretending to be alive in the Middle Ages. Pictures of a Norman baron resting his leg and saying to a fellow-baron 'I've got curtilage trouble', and of another baron handing over a Saracen to his seneschal with the words 'Please place in a dry keep', are merry and valid, because they admit and exploit anachronism, but 'Summer is a-coming in' is just flatly ignorant.

However, words in honest use are entitled to slither, dither, soar, plunge, and all but sink. I am not prating; T. S. Eliot in *Burnt Norton* makes them also strain, crack, break, slip, slide, perish, decay, and refuse to stay still or in place. The estimable housewife has degenerated into the *huzzy*, but has also depersonalised herself into the soldier's useful *hussive*; the godsibb or 'godparent' gives her title to the evil abstraction *gossip*; the *knave* was once a mere 'boy', the *quean* a 'woman'; a puisné judge is now no more *puny* than his colleagues. These highly personal words typify the way in which our speech sours and denigrates and belittles; more importantly for our subject, they show how familiar speech dictates the rules of written English, and I am accepting all through this book that this is how things should be, however little we may enjoy these radical changes in decent words. The process has also been at work in words where no moral judgement is involved, and it blunts or sharpens the edges of words that were surely adequate as they once stood. Alysoun's thirteenth-century lover, who declares that 'In hue her hair is fair enough', is not saying that he has seen worse or that it's not so dusty; what now reads like slang meant 'very lovely'. A caricatured fourteenth-century friar, who complains that 'lewd men are now so stout/That they give us neither flesh nor fish', is referring to laymen turned stately, who won't give meat or fish in alms. A *flood* was 'flowing' water, not just water in the wrong place, and *starve* was universally 'die', as it still is in the North; *near* was the comparative of *nigh*, and meant 'nearer', whereas now *nigh* is extinct in the standard tongue save in *wellnigh*, a word I have never myself used. In general, as these ancient words weakened and paled in the Middle Ages, the new French importations took over the burden of precision; the older importations, such as *just* and *very*, suffered with their English colleagues. Thus what does 'I have just run over a dog' mean?—that I have merely done so, or that I have done so this very minute? My phrase 'this very minute' is acceptable, but 'Very God of Very God' is said to be puzzling, as keeping the old meaning 'true'.

This last paragraph has been a mere but deliberate digression: there is nothing we can do, or should do, to make *silly* mean 'holy' or 'happy' again, or to recall the flat word *nice* to its old connotations of foolishness. It was a necessary digression, as showing that semantic change is not a killer disease for a language, and that twentieth-century modifications of words are all part of a process; but it does not by any means condone all our abuse of the vocabulary. The Middle Ages were handling an English which, until about 1400, largely lacked patronage, status, standardisation, and dictionaries; most speakers were illiterate, most literates had been educated through French about Latin; the wind of change blew where it listed (meaning 1, *Oxford English Dictionary*), the frail barque of our language just listed (meaning 5). As we shall witness during the course of this book, lovely speech-habits were eroded—the cadence of inflected forms, the sumptuous expedient of compounding, the strength of ancient verbs and nouns: God ceased to be *Drighten*, and *nim* (probably on everyone's tongue every day) yielded to the Norse parvenu *take*. We, on the other hand, have universal education conveyed in our own language, cultured speech available by button even if there be none in our families, books in plenty, cheap dictionaries. Our opportunities for holding on to our supple and expressive language are far stronger than they were in the fourteenth century, when the language was redeemed from its servitude, and it seems to me unpardonable that we have so maltreated words not slight or slurred but shapely, clear, and meaningful: what has come over us, to misuse *awful, terrible, tremendous, amazing, fantastic, fabulous*? A few months ago the butcher-girl apologised for delivering the meat late: 'I'm sorry—the shop's a shambles'; I felt like congratulating her on the only correct use of the word that I had ever heard. I must reserve *literally* for the deserved and especial venom of a climactic chapter, but *decimated* runs it close; any group of people or things losing any of its numbers or bulk is now said to be 'decimated', as if this had meant 'nearly destroyed'—certainly no way to run a legion. And what are we to make of a *Bristol Evening Post* advertisement in October 1964?—'Board Residence for two respectable gentlemen . . . car essential but not necessary, four miles from centre . . .'

Such handling of any language will make it prone to bloat. Its riches will be thrown away as mere excess; its lucid and distinctive words will be used with exaggeration, their outlines dulled and their picturesqueness effaced. I am not condemning inventiveness, though it might well be felt that we have plenty of words to be getting on with, and the Brownings, for example, coined rather naughtily: see consecutively the words *awaste, awatch, awave*, in the *Shorter Oxford English Dictionary*, by Elizabeth, Elizabeth, and Robert, respectively. Charles Lamb was one of the first to do this kind of thing with talent, in the melancholy and telling word *albumess*, for a doomed spinster who stayed at home pressing leaves and what not; but brilliance is

22

needed for such inventiveness, and sixth-formers who go through a period of emulating Dylan Thomas after reading *Under Milk Wood* for A-levels, or have even bolder aims after engaging with *Finnegan's Wake*, will probably achieve little more than some laboured and synthetic compounds. Let us, rather, tend what we have: it is an abundance.

Some curious ambiguities have arisen from a variety of historical accidents; it would be good if one of each pair of meanings could even now be cancelled. A striking example is the confusion of the Archbishops of Canterbury and York, as Primates, with a group that includes monkeys and lemurs; this is never likely to cause real misunderstanding. The frequent newspaper jotting of the type 'Woman Critical After Accident' will call to the callous mind a picture of her haranguing a peccant motorist. Two *Bristol Evening Post* headlines were very arresting: 'Youth's Sponge Beats Women' (November 1966)—it was in a cake competition, and 'Three CPOs confirmed' (February 1960), whereat I rejoiced to think of these three tough naval chief petty officers, not normally men of strong spirituality, presenting themselves in their maturity before the Bishop of Bristol . . . Sadly, it referred to compulsory purchase orders, and no doubt some decent old householders, without the means to pay for litigation, were being thrown out and exiled to suburban flats to make way for the sour dream of a planner. The customary newspaper report, 'Her screams attracted a passer-by', should not—but does—suggest his comment, 'Oh, you *do* scream nicely!'; and I have been assured that there was recently a brand of pastry-mix bearing the inscription 'Enough for four persons or twelve little tarts'. But in the case of serious words that have little risk of causing mirth, it is a pity that weighty and scrupulous writers so often choose a pedantic and secondary meaning; even John Harvey, a stylist, writes in *The Plantagenets* that Edward I 'betrayed both legal caution and a sense of humour' in his homage to Philip the Bold, but the context makes it clear that he displayed/revealed/showed these qualities, and the artificial use of *betrayed*, though allowed by the lexicon, obstructs and distracts the reader. And when such a word as *overlook* develops two opposite meanings—to scrutinise and to ignore—there is perhaps no gain in retaining the services of the word at all. Yet the old conflict of *let* = 'allow' and *let* = 'prevent' ('I'll make a ghost of him that lets me!') had a happy ending, with the quelling of the second but the retention of its cognate noun on passports and in some time-honoured ballgames.

I earlier discouraged the facetious use of archaisms. They can remain blamelessly in nursery rhymes—'Let me taste your ware' preserves a word that now has no official life save in compounds like *warehouse* and in the artificial limitation to crockery; we even accept a sequence of them, as when the King of Hearts 'beat the *Knave full sore*' or when the birds '*Fell a*-sighing and *a*-sobbing'. But their presence in hymns and liturgies has long caused restlessness. My education, and most of the soul of me, make me long for the retention of the Authorized Version and the Book of Common Prayer, even though the realist and evangelist in me may acknowledge a need for the New English Bible and for some 'Series' of the services, provided that the sermon be not the '*New Statesman* leader', or the choir the 'protest pop group', of the kind deprecated by Robert Conquest in an open letter to Archbishop Coggan.

But the wording of many current hymns has no strong justification on the grounds of antiquity or cadence or sheer poetry or the *mot juste*. It is notorious that children have been scared by the 'altar . . . in each man's cot', puzzled by the 'peculiar honours', and amused by the 'friendly crook' and 'sudden greens' of even so proper a poet as Addison or the 'thousands meekly stealing' and their 'faithful watches keeping' in the disorderly profusion of Faber, who also expects us to sing such cacophonies as 'earth's green fields'. It is inspiring to see how the really great hymns are still unerringly right—Samuel Crossman's 'My song is love unknown', after 300 years; Anstice's 'When came in flesh', after 150. Mrs Alexander's 'There is a green hill far away' falters in using *without* for *outside*. But even so eminent a translator as J. M. Neale was persuaded—not by his original but by a mistaken dependence on an artificial idiom—to prolong, in his 'O blest Creator of the light', the life of *o'er, meet array, eve, darkling, whelm'd, lure* (noun), and (doubly a non-idiom) *that we ask be done*; perhaps, after all, it is the Angers melody that carries this hymn along. Of course, it is impossible to do anything tuneful with *might'st* and *didst*, and many twentieth-century hymnographers and liturgiologists have profited by the new mode of addressing God as 'You' and thus avoided these difficult singular verbs. Some new forms of service, suggested or already adopted, are so radical in their use of many modern idioms that I am surprised at the archaisms that linger in them, especially the use of *that* for *so that* as the introduction to purpose-clauses, and 'from whom no secrets are *hid*', in the Series 3 of the Church of England.

I once found myself formulating an essay title as follows:

'English expression is falling between poets who exploit the penumbra of a word and philosophers who attempt pedantically to abolish it. Discuss'. I must have half-believed in this problem at the time, though essay titles don't have to be sincere; but I feel less glum about it now. Poets have every right to sound a word to its depths, and prose-writers, if willing to proceed more slowly and less elliptically, are entitled to feel, and share with us, the same excitement. When Pevsner calls the façade of the Baptist Chapel at Ridgmont 'dissolute', he takes and leads an imaginative leap which no itemised account could have set in motion. Unless we are to live in the cut-and-dried world of the banxring, the oxter, and the paxwax, we shall treasure the many grey and furry words along with those that declare themselves with immediate clarity; each new context will give them a new illumination, but their power may remain in their elusiveness. As for philosophers, I suppose they have no intrinsic right to pare a word down to one meaning, save as a pastime; many of them write with admirable definition, and many in words that could have no place in poetry, but I cannot sincerely think that our expression is errant between the opposite poles of that essay title. Our huge vocabulary awaits our responsible and individual use; we must not let sloth seduce us into using the trite, or novelty the merely different. But it is time to turn to that great storehouse of new words, the compounding of nouns.

3

THE PERILS OF THE COMPOUND NOUN

Old English, the almost entirely Germanic tongue of before 1066, used compound nouns in great numbers in both its prose and its verse. This was, and remains, a Germanic habit, as can be seen by reference to any of the extant languages of this family—German, Dutch/Flemish, Danish, Norwegian, Swedish, Icelandic, Faeroese; alone of the Germanic stock, English appears to have sloughed most of its ancient compounds and even to have largely turned from this method of word-formation. The new emphasis on phrasal expression may at first sight seem to have deprived us of many economical and expressive words; but they were satisfactory only if they were shapely and unequivocal, and perhaps a mere saving on syllables is the only thing that can be *proved* for rewriting the Psalmist's words as 'If I take the morningwings, and dwell in the uttermost seaparts'. Let us first, however, see what has happened to the family of one stem since 1066: the score of words which in Old English had *wyrt* (plant, vegetable, herb, spice; Modern English dialect 'wort') as their first element.

Of these, five had second elements now completely un-

27

recognisable, and have perished for ever. Nine others neither survive nor have equivalent compound forms using other words; but their modern spelling could have been *wortbreath* (fragrance), *wortforbearance* (restraint from action by the operation of herbs), *wortkin* (species of plant), *wortdrink* (herbal drink, medicine), *wortmeat* (pottage, dish of herbs), *wortmingling* (herbal mixture), *worttown* (garden —though Old English *tūn* has come a long way in meaning since its beginnings), *worttownhedge* (garden enclosure), *wortward* (gardener). Three are represented by compounds of the same type: *wortbed* (which is much like 'flowerbed'), *wortbox* ('pomander box', which the *Oxford English Dictionary* does not hyphenate), *wortvat* ('scentbottle'). Only one is still truly with us, and even this has not been true to its original meaning: *wortyard*, the source of our 'orchard' but literally indicating a 'kitchengarden'.

Of course, the first element in these cases is so nearly dead (save as the second element of plants such as penny-wort and stitchwort) that its decay may have involved all its compounds in ruin, but even if we examine the com-pounds of a familiar stem such as *church*, the tally will be largely of casualties. Old English had nearly forty *church*-words, but who would now attach any meaning to *churchboot* (repair of churches), *churchbreach* (sacrilege), *churchright* (church dues), *churchhood* (order in the church), *churchhallowing* (consecration of a church), *churchhater* (per-secutor), *churchneed* (requirements of a church), *churchtide* (service time), *churchtown* (churchyard), *churchthane* (minister), *churchthing* (object belonging to a church), *churchthinger* (priest), *churchwatch* (vigil), *churchweed* (vest-ment), and *churchward* (sexton—though the churchwarden is a venerable newcomer instead)? Who but an antiquarian would recognise *churchfrith* and *churchgrith* (sanctuary), *churchscot* and *churchscotwork* (the Martinmas church-due, and work in connexion with it), and *churchsoken* (church privilege or territory)? Neat little words, long perished as to their second elements, conveyed *churchmarriage* (celibacy) and *churchbusiness* (simony). Only *churchbell*, *churchbook*, *churchdoor*, *churchgoing*, *churchland*, *churchsong* and *churchsinger* can still express their original meaning; but the last two are not now real words, *churchland* is technical, and the *churchbook* was not *any* book but the missal or a similar manual.

In the case of a living stem such as *church*, a good dictionary will reveal how we have compensated for some of these losses by forming new compounds, including *church-text* (a type of lettering), *church-flag* (hoisted during a service on board), *church-owl* (the barn-owl), and exquisite technicalities such as *church-papist* for a seventeenth-century Roman Catholic who outwardly conformed; even *church-yard* is not demonstrably older than 1160. But, in general, the picture of our compound nouns since the Norman Conquest has been one of catastrophic decay in most cases, and of radical change in most others. How did it come about that we lost our ancestral habit of compounding?

It would be hard now to determine how far literate Anglo-Saxons shaped the language of their fellows, but if they were literate they could normally read Latin, and they must have noticed how very different it was from Old English in the matter of compounding, and how awkward this made things for the translator. For Latin is not at all a compounding language; nor is its derivative, French, and the subsequent arrival of the latter must have occasioned, among other changes in syntax, a weakening of the system whereby nouns were juxtaposed and given a new joint meaning. Incidentally, Classical Greek is a language of notably expressive compounds, though it had to wait its turn until the Renaissance; Welsh, which has never had its turn to influence English, compounds very little, despite the rather bogus placename in Anglesey, but gets on very well by other means. English is probably very lucky in this matter; just as our vocabulary is in two principal layers, Germanic and Romance, so we can express some noun relationships by linking them, some phrasally, and some by either method; we can cling to a few ancient forms, or dare to make exciting new ones. But let me not sound too enthusiastic about these dangerous possessions; it must be inquired first whether the double-barrelled noun is intrinsically worth having.

One of my earliest memories of a linguistic oddity dates from the unsolicited arrival through our letter-box, in my extreme childhood, of a bulb catalogue from Holland, gaudy with promise. The preface urged us to adorn our 'houserooms with gay winterpots full of all tulipsorts', and I gathered at once that the Dutch went about language in a different way from ours. The wording may have its upholders, to claim that the three compressed words are pithy and perfectly clear; but it so happens (language is full of unpredictable chances like this) that we actually have a word *houseroom* already, when we say 'I wouldn't give it houseroom!', so it cannot after all be argued that a houseroom *must* mean 'a room in a house'; a winterpot may be granted the earthy simplicity of meaning 'a pot in winter', but comparison with *flowerpot, jampot, lobsterpot, fleshpot, chamberpot, chimneypot* and *swankpot* suggests all kinds of useless and vague relationships, and absurdities such as the reflection that since a flowerpot contains flowers and not *a* flower, is a winterpot filled with winters?

And this is the disabling factor in the compound noun: that no standard exists whereby the one noun is in a fixed relation to the other. A lighthouse is a house (though not in our normal sense) with/for a light, a daymark is a conspicuous landmark for the use of seafarers by day, a lifeboat is a boat for saving life, part of a breeches-buoy resembles breeches; it may be said at once that usage has sanctioned these meanings, that no other meanings have accrued, and that each of these words is now an entity so strong that we do not mentally dismember it. But all this still gives us no warrant to form any new compound, and no clue to the relationship within an unfamiliar one; if we are ignorant of ornithology, how are we to understand that a ring-dove has a little collar, that a stock-dove lives in treestumps, and that a turtle-dove is of the genus *Turtur*? Thus unless *all* compounds are accepted as new words, with meanings to be learnt, and not as doubled old words, with meanings to be assumed, they are dangerous acquisitions. But they look impressive, and they blandish: there lies on my desk a screed, supposedly about English, which contains the words *selection-criteria* and *language-state*; its companion, more modest, uses *field-theory, project-work*, and *course-structure*. Writers nowadays seem unable to carry on without such clumsy and ill-defined words, as if bemused by their length and newness; I am not impugning the length of them—our suffixed (not compounded) word *frightfulness* is as valid and effective and logical as *Schrecklichkeit*, and *Threefoldhood* (if it existed) would be as

31

expressive as the preferred *Trinity*—but merely to put two nouns cheek by jowl does not settle them into a stable relationship: and that goes for *value-judgement*, too.

Now for something similar but worse: the piling-up of nouns, with an undefined bearing on one another, to form one vast unhyphenated noun. Fortunately, its natural habitat is in the newspaper headline, and I must generously admit that the need to save space and to catch the eye is some justification for its existence. But nothing can excuse the example in the *South Wales Echo* for 13 August 1959: SPEEDBOAT DEATH BLAZE RESCUE BID MEN PRAISED; that is seven (since *speedboat* is a compound), but even more damage is done by two in the *Bristol Evening Post* for 8 February 1962: HOT FAT BOY GETS £212 DAMAGES—it turned out that the lad was an apprentice cook on British Railways, and got a skillet of hot fat down himself when the train went over the points. It is surely not legitimate (quite apart from the daft double meaning) to associate the two nouns *fat* and *boy* and then airily let the reader guess that this is a boy who has had dripping spilt on him. Another *South Wales Echo* specimen (so venial that I have mislaid the date) was CASH PROBE RAP FOR BLAENAVON; I do not *like* the phrase, and I am glad that it has not become a familiar compound *cashprobrap*, but I admit that it is pretty clear and succinct and aptly harsh. In all these accumulations, the great wrongness goes back to our habit of compounding—and of compounding in what may well be considered the wrong order.

Outside a building of red brick in the Glamorgan town of Caerffili, I observed an eight-line, eight-word, bilingual notice, vertically planned:

YSBYTY
GLOWYR
CYLCH
CAERFFILI

CAERPHILLY
DISTRICT
MINERS
HOSPITAL

The arrangement is palindromic, chiastic: the Welsh, in precisely the opposite order to the English, says 'Hospital (of) Miners (of) District (of) Caerffili', and who would seriously assert that this order is inferior? Imagine a medical emergency: a stranger to the town rushes to the gates, but whereas if he is monoglot Welsh or bilingual he gets at once the operative word he longs for, if he is monoglot English he is first informed of the town where he is standing, secondly that the building serves a wider area, thirdly that it was built mainly with colliers in mind, and at last that it is indeed a hospital. Well may the French criticise us for saying 'Canada cod liver oil'; there is no doubt that it is more communicative to mention at once the oil which is the real substance of the phrase, and then to limit it step by step as 'oil of liver of cod of Canada'. And even German has decided that a word meaning 'speedboatdeathblazerescuebidman' is supernumerary.

One further warning: an adjective placed before two juxtaposed nouns is apparently the servant of either master. So 'Fabulous Christmas Bargains' is taken to mean fabulous (though not really) bargains for Christmas, whereas 'Continental Holiday Brochures' are

C   33

brochures for continental holidays. It is no answer to say that commonsense will guide us to the right interpretation; bargains for a wonderful Christmas and continental leaflets for holidays are both real concepts. And what of the shop's apology based on 'Temporary Assistant Shortage'?—is this a shortage of temporary assistants (I fear that we must, in either case, mentally make this plural) or a temporary shortage of assistants (whether *they* are permanent or not)? It will be realised that this seemingly pithy form of expression is always technically open to two meanings, is sometimes actually so, and is occasionally bizarre; we shall see more of its oddities when we consider the misplacing of words, and it must suffice at present to mention that waterproof gentlemen's macintoshes could not happen in a language that richly declined its adjectives.

4

CACOPHONY

There can be no language in the world that has such potential for euphony along with cacophony as has English; its music ranges from cadences and vowel harmonies and expressive consonants down to grunts and cackles. A little-heard verse of the National Anthem expects us to sing 'Frustrate their knavish tricks'—an ugly concatenation of fifteen consonants in only six syllables, and 'Saint Patrick's Breastplate', the title of one of our handsomest hymns, has fifteen in only five, including *ntp*, *ksbr* and *stpl* as neighbours; faced with such a phrase, vernacular speech slurs it to 'Sn Patrick's Breasplate', which flows a little more but is to blame for its falsification. Tonguetwisters are an enjoyable childhood pastime, as if making the best of a bad job; and we could well start by considering one, the familiar 'She sells sea-shells on the sea-shore'. This turns pretty at the end, and we hear the waves breaking and booming in the *s . . . sh . . . ore*; but the first part exemplifies one of our worst sources of cacophony—the hiss and the buzz.

By an unhappy linguistic chance, and not by choice, we are left with the rule that *all* our third person singular present indicatives, save for a few auxiliaries but including

35

is and *has,* end in a hiss (if the verb stem ends in *f, k, p, t,* or the *th* of *bath*) or (and far more frequently) in a buzz; the buzz is not, however, acknowledged, and so the 'correct' *z* is not written in this position. I have already expressed surprise that the '3rd sing. pres. indic.' should be allowed to cling to its inflexion whereas the plural, say, has none; none is needed for expressiveness, 'he go' being intrinsically as meaningful as 'I go', and furthermore why did it have to be the *s/z* sound? The standard inflexion for this part of the verb in the Middle Ages was *-eth,* and *-s* is a latish parvenu from the Northern dialect; unfortunately, it coincides in sound with another *s/z* that has arisen both fortuitously and with strong hints from French, that of almost all plural nouns. Observe at once the anomaly that plural nouns, with their *-s* ending, will, when subjects, have verbs without *-s,* and that all singular nouns, without *-s,* will have verbs with *-s;* it looks almost contrived, and we put up with it because we have become used to it. It need not have happened: the plural *-s* goes back to the *-as* plural of most of the strong masculine nouns of Old English, but a few strong masculines, all the strong feminines and neuters, all the weak masculines, weak feminines, and weak neuters, and various anomalous classes, had no such thing. (I use these regrettably vague terms 'strong' and 'weak' because they are customary. There is no need to explain them here; the uninitiated must simply observe that the Old English *-as* did not dominate the plural noun as does our *-s*). How much more beautiful and cadenced our language might have been if chance had shunted all our plural nouns off into the siding that was freighted with the 'weak' *-an!*—it is represented now only by the humble *oxen* and (with a mistaken extension) *children* and the rare *brethren*; a few elderly rustics are said to refer still to their *hosen* and *shoon*, but I have never met them. The lilting beauty of this *-en* can be epitomised by comparing 'The father loveth his children' with 'The father loves his kids'.

Am I, then, letting nostalgia get the better of me, and pleading for a return to this *-eth* and *-en*? Or are they just the spilt milk and the moon, which it is wrong to cry over and for? Well, my indictment of the hiss and the buzz is not yet over; nor is my catalogue of them and their follies: the tyranny of the Old English strong masculine nouns (and, in this case, of the strong neuters as well) imposed on us another and much nastier *s/z*, their genitive singular going back to Old English *-es*. Now the former *-as* plural became *-es* and thereafter in most cases *-s*; but the former *-es* genitive has been curiously distinguished—it has, unlike the plural, had its dropped *e* commemorated by an apostrophe, and so *'s* has come to seem to us the mark of possession or attribution or some vaguer form of reference. This may seem to some a handy spelling convention, though the use of it in words such as *uncle's* is absurd, this genitive having been *uncles* already and not *unclees*. But worse followed: the *s/z* sound was applied to plurals also, as a sign of possession, with no basis whatever in Old English, and then the silly trick started whereby *-s'* means possession in the plural. No one can say what has been left out where that final apostrophe stands, and of course nothing has; but it is pretended that we have three distinct declined forms in nearly all our nouns—*princess's, princesses, princesses'*. Yet all three are sounded exactly alike; it is a misfortune for any language when the written forms make assertions so different from those made by the pro-

37

nunciation, and in most respects English has prudently or luckily avoided having two forms, spoken and literary, so that this anomaly is both regrettable and surprising.

However, the disaster area is even wider. The custom arose (and for no historical reasons) of limiting possession by -'s to animates only, until it sounded right to say *the boy's hat* and *the brim of the hat*, and wrong to say *the hat of the boy* and *the hat's brim*. Like so many rules, this has obvious exceptions such as *the river's edge* or *Journey's End*, along with many obscured ones such as *once* (formerly an 'adverbial' genitive *ones*, and followed less legitimately by *twice* and the moribund *thrice*) and *needs* in 'needs must'; but though we accept that a simple inanimate cannot normally 'possess' in -'s, we have to insist that it *must* when it is a component in a phrase such as is found in 'I strongly object to the matter's being discussed behind closed doors', because here we remember that *being* is a noun and must therefore be preceded by a 'genitive', a 'possessive': 'Do you object to my smoking?', not 'Do you object to me smoking?' Now, admittedly, this rule is formally sound; admittedly, too, I have pleaded for the retention of inflexions and even, wistfully, for their extension, and shall plead for it again. But there can be a peculiar ambiguity in such a spoken sentence as 'In many theatres there is a risk of the audience in the boxes'/box's seeing only half the stage' (in one box or more?), and a peculiar ugliness when the 'possessing' phrase is longwinded: 'There has been complaint of the indiscriminate felling of undergrowth in the park's causing a disturbance in wild life.' There is only one way to sort out this kind of sentence: avoid altogether the idiom that involves the verbal noun in -*ing*, and reconstruct the sentence at greater length and

38

with total clarity. After all, the wretched process whereby our old present participles in *-nd/-nde* and our old verbal nouns in *-ng* have fallen together in sound and in spelling and (to some: 'Do you object to me smoking?') in meaning has made the verbal noun into a thing to be handled nervously. Used when a verb should be used instead, it is in principle objectionable and in effect harmful; used as a real noun, it is in the hands of poets a splendid thing:

The rising of the sun, and the running of the deer,
The playing of the merry organ, sweet singing in the
choir.

The verbal noun preceded by a clumsy phrase ending in -'*s* makes it obvious that, in any case, this possessive inflexion should not be too far separated from the real possessor. How much more sensible it is to clear the ground with a plain sentence 'My cousin in the technical section of the reference library has a fiancée' than to economise with a phrase such as 'the fiancée of my cousin in the technical section of the reference library' (she or he could be in it) or, worse, 'my cousin in the technical section of the reference library's fiancée' (where an impossible relationship is adumbrated)! I suppose that on the model of that third version 'the fiancée of my cousin in Woolworth's' would be 'my cousin in Woolworth's's fiancée', and 'my cousin in Guinness's's' is quite feasible. In such cases, the use of the phrase with *of* is the only proper procedure.

Hypnotised by the importance of -'*s*, those who display notices in public often use this form in preference to the simple plural; TEA's is not uncommon, and another kind of blunder occurs in the frequent LADIE'S HAIRDRESSER. The ignorant add -*s* indiscriminately to the present indicative of verbs, as if there weren't enough already: *I goes, you goes, we goes, they goes*; and we also have a formidable set of hissing suffixes in -*ess*, -*less*, -*ness*, -*ous*, -*ose*, as well as the buzzing -*ise* (which I prefer to spell in a manner more Greek and phonetic, with -*ize*, but fashion outvotes me). Small wonder that he who had 'the finest ear' of our poets, Tennyson, systematically went through his verses and cut out all the sibilants he could; but in the heat of conversation we can hardly be so careful, and that other -'*s*, the reduced form of both *is* and *has*, adds its buzz to the gritty monosyllables: 'That man's dog's bitten me' must surely be a commoner spoken form than one with the full *has*, and 'My son is going to college' is certainly far rarer than 'My son's'.

Between them, our sibilants and our over-abundant monosyllables occasion most of the cacophony. I must add at once that monosyllables well chosen and well placed are not a greater danger than are florid polysyllables, and in the hands of a responsible poet such as A. E. Housman, who revised and excised and polished diligently, their cold power is tremendous; it happens that he was our greatest Classical scholar, so that he had polysyllables in profusion to draw on if he wished, but the words that he put into the mouths of the dead in war are these:

Here dead lie we because we did not choose
    To live and shame the land from which we sprung.
Life, to be sure, is nothing much to lose;
    But young men think it is, and we were young.

Only two words here have more than one syllable, the native *nothing* and the half-exotic *because*, and they would hardly be called rare or flowery (to most speakers, *because* is a monosyllable, *cos*); yet the stanza has a practised precision, clarity, dignity, and melody. Even the humble preposition and conjunction, usually thought of as not 'operative', can assume much greater vitality and independence when a poet is making every word count. Christopher Ricks in a recent essay on Wordsworth (in *Harvard English Studies*, 2) reminds us that these little old words are the 'humble fundamentals' without which 'the simplest and most permanent forms of language' are inexpressible; further, 'if as a poet you are concerned above all with relations and relationships, you are bound to give special importance to those words which express relationship: prepositions and conjunctions'. But whereas a poet can give such authority to even the slightest word, speakers and writers today commonly slur them, agglomerating with the preposition the short adverb also, as if for reinforcement; hence phrases, expressive of nothing extra, such as 'I met up with him' or 'I'll check up on that' or 'You'll have to face up to it', in neither of which there is need of the adverb or even of the preposition. The probably apocryphal nurse who had to read to her scholarly patient, and who at length burst out with 'What do you want to pick on a book like this to be read to from out of with for?', did not exclaim in vain if her example can still warn us not to throw away valid words.

It is hard to give practical advice based on this chapter. Many of our commonest nouns and verbs are short and brutish, and it is too late to reshape them; their residual ugliness has often come with age. We have little time in what we must write, and even less in what we must say, to frame vowel harmonies or handsome cadences; but at least we should all try to speak articulately, beginning with *yes* for *yeah* and working steadily up through *very* for *ve'y* (or the frequent *ve'y-ve'y*) to elaborate conventions like *What is the matter with you?* for *Wossamarrawijoo?*, which lacks concern. It strikes me that the best formula for clear and harmonious writing is found in a well written letter; I have already said that English is fortunate in not having two languages, spoken and literary, and a good letter, spontaneous yet composed, meant to interest and convince and inform and cheer a loved or respected friend, is the meeting-place of logic and music, mind and soul, detachment and subjectivity, speech and prose. Ideally, our speech to persons should reproduce the ways of a good personal letter; a good personal letter should directly reflect our sincere speech. But, of course, letter-writing has decayed; its last flowering was in World War II, but many factors—including the incidence of telephones—have worked against it, and it is little engaged in even as a pastime.

5

THE GAPS AND PITFALLS IN OUR GRAMMAR

What can be said in defence of a language when it allows as equivalents the sentences 'The best thing he does is sing', 'The best thing he does is sings', 'The best thing he does is to sing', and 'The best thing he does is singing'? It will by now seem clear that English goes to work with a bursting vocabulary still capable of expansion, with a varied set of musical effects, and with an apparent simplicity, but that all this has to be articulated by a slender and rickety grammatical system. Only on the grounds of lilt and flow do I claim that the straightforward sentence 'The good lads went to the black mill' is inferior to what would be the Chaucerian version, 'The goode laddes wenten to the blake melle', where the three sounded final -e inflexions stand respectively for a plural adjective, a weak adjective after a definite article, and a dative noun. But where the constructions are more elaborate, and where a disarray is enforced or seems desirable, the grammatical framework—absolutely sound in the modern sentence which I have exhibited—will often be inadequate. I called our grammar 'slender and rickety'; indeed, there is little of it, and some of *that* has almost fallen to pieces.

43

Yet we are not, it appears, constitutionally opposed to inflexions—at least, if our present liking for suffixes is anything to go by. We are showing an insane love even of pure inflexions such as those whereby nouns create verbs (prócessing, card-indexed), and the blurred noun suffixed in *cowmanship* or *gamesmanship* has resulted in many of these popular but clumsy forms; worst of all is *-wise* (another *z*) in *financewise* and all its limitless cousins. Similarly, we affix *pre-*, *pro-*, *ante-* and *anti-* (a regrettable pair of un-identical twins) with little regard for the sound or length of the resulting word. But in general the old inflexional system has fallen away; and even when a really distinctive 'irregular' inflected form still stands out from its fellows, it may be subjected to analogical 'levelling', whereby a fragment of the old grammar is made to conform, shall we say, to a comprehensive system. The chief casualties here are the old 'strong' verbs, which changed their stem vowels to form their past tenses and past participles, and did not, as did the 'weak', add a dental suffix. Every new borrowed or formed verb is made to fit into the weak conjugation—we do not say *I telephone, I telephane, I have telephene*; but *strive* was long ago taken from French and 'mistakenly' fitted to the pre-existing habits of *drive*, and *catch* was taken from French and made irregular weak, with a dental suffix but also a change of stem vowel. Who, then, is 'right' about these two verbs?—he who follows the almost unbroken rule and says *I strived, I have strived, I catched, I have catched*, or he who adopts the inexplicable forms *strove, striven, caught*? Everything refutes the behaviour of *strive*, and the normal process, which has been going on for hundreds of years, is to make the strong verb weak; in journalism, the rugby player has often *weaved* in

44

and out of his opponents, and at last the 'correct' *strived* seems to be asserting itself. Lest you be thinking 'What harm is there in this?', observe what happens when such a process takes place: the three characteristic parts of the strong verb (say, *spin, span, spun*) are reduced to two (*spin* and—with two functions—*spinned: spin, spun, spun* is already current), and it is tempting to assume from the identity of the two past forms that their functions are identical, too. This has proved catching, and *I seen him* and *I done it* are among the commonest faults of speech. Even educated people say *we sung* (the *u* was formerly correct in the plural, but it occurs now because *sang* has been tainted by the past participle); and there must often be alternative forms in the minds of careless speakers. A man who will say *I'ld've knowed him straight away* would not dream of saying anything but *well known*. It seems to me that the now popular forms such as *drink, drunk, drunk* achieve nothing more than would their complete capitulation to the weak conjugation as *drink, drinked, drinked*. So nearly complete is the regularising process, that we find it exceptionally funny to form a new past tense of *grin* such as *I grun*, or (an old High Church joke) to say *The Vicar praught*. We would regard as ignorant anyone who said *I teached*, and as eccentric anyone who said *I raught out my hand*; but both forms once had the *-aught* spelling, and only caprice has preferred the irregular in one case and the analogical in the other. It so happens that even *to wear* was once a weak verb, making *wear, weared, weared* historically 'correct'; but the combined influence of *bear, swear* and *tear* overbore it.

Among the very worst of our verbs are the blurred *put, put, put,* and the similar repetitions of *cut, set, hit,* and *let,*

45

where only context can fix the tense as present or past, though golf allows *putted*; the Americans have certainly kept a more expressive form than the British in *get, got, gotten*—this ugly monosyllabic verb is much improved by the disyllable, and *buy, bought, boughten* deserves general adoption, too. But because almost all our past tenses and past participles have fallen together into one form with a dental suffix, the risk of ambiguity in the telescoped English of headlines is very great: 'Doctor Threatened to Get Purple Hearts', said one—*did* he, or *was* he? 'Student Refused Vac Job', said another; was this indolence, or anti-student discrimination? Incredibly, the same Bristol newspaper allowed a choice between a past tense and an imperative in 'Set Fire to Man's Flat, Court Told', and between a noun and a third person plural present indicative verb in 'Service Families Need Decreases'.

Of course, it is this same blurring of inflexions that helps to fix the wonderful aptitude of English for humour; the ease with which we may substitute one part of speech for another, the ubiquitous -*s*, and the studied brevity of our wit, are all factors in this. The Victorian riddle, 'What is the difference between the death of a sculptor and the death of a hairdresser?' (Answer: One makes faces and busts, and the other curls up and dyes), exploits its ambiguities somewhat tediously; Dr Spooner, and those who invented most of his remarks, are rather more dependent on the strange riches of our vocabulary, whereby a pub called The Dull Man at Greenwich becomes almost as credible as one called The Green Man at Dulwich. In such infelicities as 'a man with one leg called Jones', a lacing of callousness adds its toll of spice. Some 'failure of communication' stories just use the otherwise regrettable ambiguities of our word-stock: 'Motorist: *Excuse me, would you like a lift?*—Lady: *No, thank you, we live in a bungalow*' is (though unfunny in America) an eminent example of this method, as are the many variations of 'He: *Shall I call you a taxi?*—She: *You might as well; you've called me everything else*' and 'Diner: *I feel like a boiled owl.*—Waiter: *I'm sorry, sir, we haven't any today*'. Though not myself greatly given to spoonerisms, I once said 'Tringle, Sing, please' on a Hertfordshire 'bus; and a clear failure of communication occurred recently when a woman student appeared at my door and I said 'Your name escapes me', to which she replied 'No—what made you think it was Catesby?' These are minor linguistic joys, but none the less real.

Let us be wholly serious again. Anyone who knows various other languages could easily draw up a wistful list of grammatical *desiderata* for English, and I shall mention a couple now, though only as a preliminary to that great want in our language, an efficient auxiliary verb system. We have a singular definite article, *the*, and—in the same form—a plural definite article; yet we have only a singular indefinite article, *a* or *an*. We feel the plural of *a man* to be, according to context, just *men* or *some men* (*some* in itself is a mighty strange word, which once conveyed oneness as in its Norse-derived cognate *same*, the Latin *semel* and *simul-*, and the Greek *hama-* and *homo-*), but we never quite establish what we mean even by *a man*: it can be a real known man, or a man as representative of the human race, or an unidentified member of a series of men, as in 'Husband: *It says in this paper that a man is run over every day in Glasgow.*—Wife: *Nonsense—he couldn't stand it*'. Our resourceful language cannot cover the niceties of

47

the statement in so few words, and needs much fuller explanation. Likewise, in the familiar jingle 'Matthew, Mark, Luke and John,/Bless the bed that I lie on', is *Bless* imperative or subjunctive or indicative?—are the Four Evangelists being told to bless, or is it hoped that they will bless, or is it stated that they *do* bless?

Our verb participles masquerade as adjectives, but haphazardly. Thus an active present participle can be used adjectivally (*He is a coming man*), but a passive present participle thus used is unthinkable (*He is a being victimised man*), and instead we must say *He is a victimised man*; but this is not clear—is the victimisation complete or continuing? We guess that a *wounded* man has suffered the wound already, once and for all, and that a *worried* man is still subject to worry, but there is no grammar to aid our choice. In the past participles, it is all opposite: no active transitive one can be used adjectivally, but the passive can (with, as we have just seen, two senses—past and present); we cannot say that one who was in the past a promising scholar is *a promised scholar*, and even intransitive uses such as *Arrived at the station, I made for my hotel* are no longer idiomatic.

I have already censured the coalescence into -*ng* of the old verbal noun in -*ng* and the present participle in -*nd*/-*nde*. Quite apart from the new solecisms like 'Do you object to me smoking?', this merger has led to many hyphenated words, with their first element in -*ing*, which are ambiguously either compound nouns, or present participles run together with nouns (and these latter should certainly *not* be hyphenated). The *Oxford English Dictionary* stipulates the spellings *acting-captain*, *acting-manager*, though admitting that the first element is a participle; but really their

48

shoeing-smith has no more right to his hyphen than has a *galloping major*. The same dictionary calls the first part of *rocking-horse* a 'ppl.', in which case it no more deserves a hyphen than does a *neighing horse*; but the fact is that this is either darkly a horse for rocking (noun) with, or a horse that rocks, and the hyphen might in the first interpretation be correct. So we are left with rocking-stones (which rock) and stepping-stones (which don't step), and this anomaly would never have existed if a form *rockend-stones* could have remained.

But, alas, the old present participle is dead, and its coevals to which we tenuously cling are not understood and not particularly useful. Among nouns, the old feminine genitive singular without -*s* survives in *Friday, Lady Day, ladybird, ladysmock* (the last three commemorating the Blessed Virgin); the -*e* of a dative singular noun in the phrasal word *alive*; the uninflected genitive singular of a noun of kinship in *mother tongue*; the dative plural (once -*um*) in *whilom* (which nobody uses), *seldom*, and numerous placenames like *Hanham* ('at the rocks') near Bristol, and surnames like *Byron* ('at the cowsheds'); the genitive singular of weak nouns, once -*an*, in *Sunday* and *Monday* (literally 'Sun's day' and 'Moon's day'), both of which have lost an -*n* in the middle; the feminine suffix -*ster* in *spinster* and in words and names now fully male, like *tapster* and *Baxter*; the genitive plural (here from -*ra*) in *Childermas* (which everyone calls Holy Innocents' Day); the accusative of reference in *nothing daunted*. The few 'weak' plurals in -*en*, supplemented by the folkculturist's word *treen* for objects of wood, and by the few old rustic ladies with their hosen and shoon, are joined in their irregularity by the few remaining plurals with mutated

D   49

vowels (*men*, *teeth*, etc) and the few former neuters that make their plurals without -*s* (like *deer* and *sheep*). Seen thus in one paragraph, this looks a rich and expressive tally of survival; but these are all museum pieces, and our real bewilderment at them is shown by our treatment of *brēc*, the old mutated plural of *brōc* ('trouser')—the version *breech* meant a pair of trousers, *breeches* must have four legs, and a pair of them presumably eight.

Similar oddities are embedded in our verbs: the negative verb in *willy-nilly* ('If I want, if I don't want'), the subjunctive in the speech-habits of anyone who says *please* (from 'if it please you') or *if I were you* or *I vote that he be elected*, the Old Norse reflexive infinitive (of all strange things!) in *bask* ('bath oneself'), the absolute construction in *during the afternoon* ('the afternoon lasting'), and various archaisms of -*eth* and -*en*. Thus a great English school proudly displays the motto *Manners Maketh Man*; the observant, used to their 1611 Bible and its consistent singular verb in -*eth*, will find this plural one very strange (it was, in fact, a Southern dialect feature), and detractors of the Public School system will mistake the original meaning of *manners* and assume that deportment and table-manners are being recommended. This word has radically changed its meaning; others remain in their original meanings, but only when supported by a limited set of adjectives or when compounded. So Old English *bēam* 'tree' has shifted in meaning to 'plank', but limps on in *hornbeam* and in G. M. Hopkins's *wind-beat whitebeam*; Old English *gamen*, reduced to our form 'game', is still entire (though disguised) in *backgammon*; *deal* ('part, share', really) is now helpless without *good*, *great*, etc, save in cutting wood or cards, or in dialect forms such as *a deal of trouble*. The childhood rhyme beginning 'If ifs and ans were pots and pans' is really about the eschewing of doubtful hypotheses, since *an(d)* could formerly mean 'if'; and the venerable *let* at tennis goes back to an Old English verb *lettan* and to a meaning which is the reverse of our verb *let* 'allow'. There is nothing intellectual about any of these archaisms: even acclimatised Americanisms such as *kerplonk* (which I hope my readers use very little) go back to Dutch, but without any spirit of antiquarian research.

What a pity it is that *thou, thee, thy, thine* and *thyself* have been finally quelled! They cling on only among a few dialect-speakers, even urban Bristolians but chiefly country folk; among those who resist the new Bibles and liturgies, the new version of the Lord's Prayer, and the trendy hymns—all of which make God 'You'; and among the oldest Quakers. For the Society of Friends at one time had the salutary custom of letting every individual person, whatever his 'rank', be singular, leaving the plural *you/your* forms for more than one person: a wholly reasonable rule, and certainly a less invidious one than the medieval convention of *thou* to an inferior, *ye* to a superior, and either to different kinds of equal. I am refreshed to read a gentle letter written by Amelia Opie in 1836, and now in my collection, with the whole panoply of *thou, thee, thy, thyself*, and I regret that the Society has largely let this distinction lapse. Looked at coolly, it is preposterous that we still have *I/we, he/they, she/they, it/they*, but no *thou/you* (*ye*, of course, has perished beyond revival); our method of addressing single and plural people by the same pronoun is clumsy, but at least is not cluttered with the etiquette and protocol that beset address in French, Spanish, German, the Scandinavian languages, and even egalitarian

Russian. I am sorry that God has officially ceased to be 'Thou'; surely He alone could have been left this distinguishing pronoun, and many Christians, old and young, in the English-speaking world will defy authority and still think and pray with this more intimate and yet more elevated form of address in their minds.

Well, we have lost many words, verbs included, since the Middle Ages; we have added thousands of new ones; we have drastically altered the meanings of many; we have shed many of the inflexions which told of the relationships of words; the pronunciation of sounds, and the stress of words, have suffered huge shifts. Now some of the changes involved matter very little, and can be a happy proof of the organic and adaptable nature of language; but one upheaval and resettlement has proved to be a seismic disaster felt throughout the whole written and spoken language—the misadventure of our auxiliary verb system.

6

THE RUINS OF OUR
AUXILIARY VERBS

I am not being nostalgic: even in Chaucer's golden time
our declaration of tense, mood and voice was far from
foolproof; but, using the same auxiliaries to different purpose, we have erected a system imprecise, cacophonous,
inconsistent, longwinded, with every inducement to slurring and with apparent riches that turn out to be pointless
alternatives. It is hard to know where to begin on a catalogue of these vital little verbs and their failings; anywhere
will suit, because everything has gone wrong.

Middle English managed nicely without an inflected
future tense, and even without a periphrastic one: 'I go
to London tomorrow' was adequate, though *will/shall*
eventually took over; but this latter was in itself a sub-
stantial change, since *will* had meant 'want/wish/intend/
mean to' and *shall* had meant 'must'. So 'I will go to heaven
when I shall die' would have conveyed both pious hope
and a recognition of necessity; but what have we done with
the ruins of *shall* and *will*? Between them, they convey a
simple future, with the fatuous rule that *shall* is for first
persons and *will* for second and third persons, except
when orders are being given—and then they change

places. I have always felt sympathy and admiration for the legendary Frenchman who fell into the Thames and shouted 'I will drown, and no one shall save me' (*and so they left him*, said the anecdote); he was a shining example to us. Our rule calls for simple reform, with *will* as the future and *shall* perishing or fighting it out with *must*. The ridiculous use of *will* for present habit ('He'll read for hours while we watch the telly') and present certainty ('If Ernest was your father, your mother will be Aunt Polly'— dead, yet apparently future and present as well as past) must be mentioned and condemned; anyway, the two ill-treated words are customarily reduced in speech to a common '*ll*.

Both had past tenses, and formally they still have; but *would* and *should* are in an even worse mess than they. Except in reported speech ('He said he would'), any sense of *would* as a future-in-the-past defeats us; in fact, its past tense is as in 'When I lived in Bognor, I would visit my aunt every day' (alternatively, 'I visited', 'I used to visit', even 'I was visiting'), but its normal use is in the present looking to the future, as a 'conditional'. Here there are inhibitions, including a weakening adherence to the *sh-*, *w-*, *w-* rule for the three persons; even as we say 'I would like' we wonder whether it ought to be 'I should like'. But *should* has come to convey moral obligation; it isn't as hectoring as *shall* or *must*, but it twists the arm. And sometimes, if unwilling to commit ourselves, we say 'I would think so' or 'I should think so' instead of 'I think so'; you see, *would* is safe and gingerly—it is not so presuming to say 'Would you be so kind?', or 'Could you be so kind?', as to say 'Will you be so kind?', though I must say that the 'Could' form, expressing bare possibility, ought to sound insulting. Of course, I have largely flattered *should* and *would* by spelling them out: to most speakers they are *'ld*, with the *l* silent. The past conditional is frankly *I'ld've* and not *I should have*, and I retain the *l* only because *'d* has normally to serve for *had*; semi-illiterates even write *I would of*, which is not surprising. Worse has followed the ease with which the elaborate periphrasis can be pronounced and mumbled; the development deserves, for its folly, its own little paragraph.

It is now deplorably normal for a sentence like 'If he had known, he would have gone' to be both slurred and expanded into 'If he'd've known, he'ld've gone'. This must stop.

The auxiliaries *have* and *had* have played a less sinister part than have some; the perfect and pluperfect tenses which they mediate are still expressive, and even *I had had* is, though ugly, logical, but it is a pity that *has* in its auxiliary use is normally pronounced as -*'z*—it thus falls together with the normal pronunciation of *is*. Unfortunately, it seems that the frequency of auxiliary *have* has weakened the force of transitive *have*, and many speakers eke this out with the nasty verb *got*; *I have got* hardly occurs, but *I've got* is frequent and *I got* (present tense) lamentably so. This, again, must stop; after all, there is no sense in saying 'She's got blue eyes', as if they had been recently acquired from elsewhere, and no sense in using the periphrasis at all. Yet it has affected the other (regrettably other) *have/had* idiom, of compulsion expressed in such a sentence as *I have to go* or *I had to see you*, and even these are therefore turned into *I've got to go* or *I'd got to see you*. Further convolutions come from another use of *have/had*—in the sense of 'get (something done)'; *I had my hair cut* gives no trouble, but *the house that I had painted* means either that the speaker had painted it or that he engaged someone to do the job. Champions of *have to* could argue that the past tense *had to* serves as the missing past tense of *must*, once a past tense and now a word which in its strict limitation of meaning is one of the least blameworthy of the auxiliaries (though on the lips of many speakers 'I *must* say' means 'There's no need for me to say this, but I'm malignantly glad of the opportunity').

If only *may* and *might* had been so modest in their scope! With the final decay of the present and past subjunctive, they took over the burden, though with no precise ruling on their duties. So *He suggested that I might go, He suggested that I should go, He suggested that I went, He suggested my going*, even *He suggested that I go*, are accepted as equivalents—an absurd state of affairs. Even in main clauses, *may* and *might* are no more satisfactory: *I may go* suggests possibility, *I might go* remote possibility; but *You might help me* can hint that 'It's the least thing you could do'. Parents who tell their children the difference between 'Can/Could I have another piece of cake?' (physical capacity) and 'May/Might I have another piece of cake?' (permission) are fighting a losing battle with these flighty words. Further strange anomalies occur: 'I might have been misinformed' and 'I could have been misinformed' seem equally correct, but the present tense allows only *may* and not *can*.

Ought remains fairly faithful to its one charge, but was not originally appointed to it. It was the past tense of a verb *owe*, which at one time conveyed not only material and moral indebtedness but also ownership, a bewildering situation palliated by adopting for the latter meaning the cognate verb *own*. But *ought* no longer means 'owed/owned'; it has present application, whereby *ought to* equals *should*, and of course a past form like *oughted* would be unthinkable, since *ought* (like *must*) is past already, so *ought to have* has to serve instead. Indeed, words such as *ought* and *must* are inconveniently deprived of other parts; thus though *I have to go* could find its way into the phrase *having to go*, no *oughting to go* is available as an alternative to *I ought to go*, or *musting* for *must*.

The verb *to be*, our one gaudily irregular verb (would there were more!—it was so enjoyable to learn *fero, ferre, tuli, latum*), performs its massive job adequately: 'I am British' (from birth), 'I am thirty' (for the first time), 'I am thirsty' (though normally my thirst is slaked), 'I am a hungry man' (habitually), 'I am eating my breakfast' (active), 'I am eaten by cannibals' (passive); we have become used to these, though their subtle or radical differences impose a great burden on the verb and on those who use it. And it has been taken further: 'I am sending my aunt a present' is a clear indication of a single future action, not of a continuous present one, whereas 'I am reading Milton' declares a process that has happened, is happening, and will continue to happen. Newspapers add their titbit to the tally of functions: 'Stroud Women are Fined for Shoplifting' could suggest to the tidy mind that all females from this harmless town spend all their days incurring such a penalty. In fact, although I said just now that *be* and its parts do a big job adequately, their performance is adequate only because our dulled senses have eventually accepted a second-best system, and because not much ambiguity arises from sentences of the kind that I quoted in illustration. Yet remember how prone is the *be* family to slurring; even quite nice people say 'Yer joking', *was* is usually rendered *wuz*, and though I still smile at the thought of the Bristol gasman who objected to the short-wave radio in his van because 'They knows where you'm to', I accept and even, in unguarded moments, use the deplorable 'Aren't I?', which is no more excusable a mixing of persons than is 'you'm' or 'they knows'. The *r* has perished from *are* and *were*, as most people pronounce them, so that I actually flattered speakers by spelling the *r* in 'Yer joking'. Thus the average Briton expresses most of his facts relating to state, identity, habit, things continuing, things suffered, and much else, in sentences that hinge on all-important words now sadly reduced to *'m*, *'z*, *'ə* (the second vowel of *murder*), *wə*, *wəz*, and similar grunts.

I ought to have mentioned earlier the *going to* idiom that expresses the future; it is fairly innocuous, but ugly in *I'm going to go* and ambiguous in *I'm going to see my aunt at Christmas*, where she or the speaker could be the visitor. But I do not care for *come to* at all; nor did the originator of 'Old Gentleman: *How did you come to fall in the harbour?* —Little Boy: *I didn't come to fall in the harbour; I came to fish*'. There is little merit in either of these misuses of *go* and *come*, verbs that have a big enough job to do already. A nasty variant of *She's come to be a big girl* is *She's got to be a big girl* or even *She's got a big girl*, as if, in the first case, it was compulsory or, in the second case, she possessed a large female offspring. As for the immediate future conveyed in *about to*, I suspect that its services have been retained through the influence of Latinists who wanted an equivalent of the *-urus* participle; but at least it is not bedevilled by any rival meaning.

This chapter is growing monotonous: it is meant to. I want to express the full dulness of the grunts and murmurs by which we try to pinpoint tense and mood and voice. But although adopting a desultory method, I have been systematic in one particular: I have kept the worst until the last—*do*. This deplorable little syllable, whose only enrichments are to the laconic forms *does* ('duz', though some despised dialect-speakers gamely improve this to 'dooz'), *did*, *done*, *doing*, has been loaded with a variety of duties that were, and could still be, far better undertaken by other constructions. It has, of course, a legitimate transitive use to denote performing or making, as in *Do your best* or *Do your homework*, and an intransitive one for behaving, as in *You have done well*; it early developed a meaning 'put', which we precariously retain in *done to death* and, facetiously, in *don* and *doff*, telescoped forms of *do on* and *do off*. Other meanings have come and gone, or remain in fossilised phrases such as *How do you do?*, which we could hardly report as *I asked him how he did*—and *how he was doing* suggests something different, relating to business; then there is the familiar *That will do* (but the past tense is not *That did*), and you can do the Trossachs, or do your trusting clients, or do your Latin prose into English. These time-honoured uses—and there are more —are complicated further by the many idioms involving an adverb or a preposition, such as *do away with*, *do up*, *done in*, *done for* in its catastrophic and its lodging-house senses, and *do without*. Now all these are idioms which have grown up organically with the language, the brevity of *do* recommending itself to lazy speech; it is certainly too late, and it would perhaps be silly, to wish any of them away, but our subject is not these finite verbs but the auxiliary

59

verb, and this is where *do* acts like a little villain. First, and only on the fringe of auxiliary use, it has long been employed as a substitute verb, whereby repetition of some other verb is avoided; whether *do* is prettier than repetition is debatable, but *Why don't you dress like other boys do?* is the form that we have grown used to. (Relentless digression, to hammer home the ugliness of our little verbs: my clause *that we have grown used to* was a concession to familiar speech, which shrinks from *to which we have grown used*; but over-familiar speech flies to *got* again, and produces *that we've got used to*. And how unpleasant a phrase *used to* is!—colliding, as it does, with the expression of past habit, *I used to beat my wife*, that inadequate idiom which now no longer has a present tense equivalent such as *I use to beat my wife*; this is just as well, since the *-d* is never sounded and *used to* is pronounced exactly the same, by most speakers, as *use to*.)

Now for the real perfidy of *do*. There was a time in our language when, to make a verb negative, you put *not* after it; this was so reasonable, so obvious, so neat, so brief, that we must feel wonder and disgust at its passing. Apart from the auxiliary verbs, only the verb *to be* consistently keeps it: *I am not the man I was*. Formally, *to have* is similar, but when can we hear in full *I have not any money* rather than *I haven't* or *I have no* or *I've not got* or *I haven't got*? When we answer *I think not*, it is not so as to indicate that we have suspended our thought-processes, but to say 'no' to an idea —*I think (that it is) not (so)*; *I hope not* is likewise elliptical, along with *I trust not* and *I fear not*, which certainly is not meant to suggest indomitable courage. No, the idiom is dead, save for the verb *to be* (except in the imperative) and for those faithful poets who still urge:

> Speak not, whisper not.
> Here groweth thyme and bergamot.

Otherwise, the long-winded and ugly periphrasis with *do* has taken over: *Don't do as I do—do as I tell you* or *She doesn't love me any more* (and *doesn't* is a particularly ill-favoured noise). Even *to be* has succumbed in its imperative: *Be not afraid* belongs only to the Bible now, and we must say *Don't be afraid*.

Well, that was bad enough; but there is worse to follow. In that same happy age when we sensibly said *I know you not*, we asked questions by reversing the order of subject and verb: *Why weep ye by the tide, ladie?* Here, again, the auxiliaries and the verb *to be* continue this habit: *Am I my brother's keeper?*—and likewise *to have*, once the *got* idiom is avoided: *Have you any money?* (Here American English often takes a step in what I consider the wrong direction, with its *Do you have the time?*). All other interrogatives are in wretched dependence on *do*: *Do you see what I mean?* Even *to do* itself is not immune from these two parasitic idioms; thus there is now no other normal way of saying *I don't do too much* or *Do you do your washing every week?* And as if all these encroachments were not enough, *do* has a strange function of emphasis when combined with another verb: *Do show me; I do so want to see it.* Thus it has invaded the negative, the interrogative, the imperative, and even the affirmative, of almost every verb—small wonder that it monopolises the interrogative negative as well: *Don't you think it's nice?*

Should I be blamed for my wrath at this wanton destruction of valid idioms?—and for wishing that we could legislate, academise, coerce, back into a pristine purity of

61

speech? I invite you to share my distaste at spat little expressions like *He's doing his thing* or lyrics (so they are called) with sentiments like

> I don't know why I love you like I do.
> I don't know why; I just do.

Now all the preceding would be more nearly endurable if the fibre of our sentences, the roots and stems around which the little auxiliaries twine and dart in their in-dispensable functions, were great shapely verbs, un-ambiguous, clearly enunciated, fit companions for the opulent and expressive nouns of which we have so many. But, no!—not content with having a homely and likeable (though thinly conjugated) verb *put*, with the sense of *place/locate*, we grossly over-use it by attaching adverbs to it and pretending (fortified by the no-nonsense claim that this is how idioms happen, and so why use high-falutin words?) that the *put* sense is still there or latent. So we put up with things instead of tolerating/enduring/suffering/tholing them, we put off instead of embarking, we are put out without having moved an inch, and we put off an appointment by a glance at our diary; we feel put off or put on, and the feelings are similar; it is notorious that Britons cannot bear to admit that they have had their pets killed, but only put down or put away or, of course, put to sleep. Well, there are other verbs as small and unsubtle as *put*, and their adaptation to cover far more elaborate concepts may seem to many, as it does to me, a failure from the start.

7

OUR INJUDICIOUS CHOICE OF
A STANDARD DIALECT

People who speak Standard Accepted English, even if they
speak it as nicely as can be, must still remember that
they are speaking merely a dialect. Its historical basis is to
be found in the little recorded Mercian of the period before 1066, and in the rather meagre and unattractive body
of East Midland literature thereafter, until in the second
half of the fourteenth century East Midland gets very
showy publicity in the works of Chaucer, his friend Gower,
the reformer Wyclif, the translator of 'Mandeville', and
others; these admired, or at least read, authors helped to
confirm the status of a prosperous regional dialect that
obtained in the rich grain and wool lands of East Anglia,
in Oxford and Cambridge, in a string of ports from London
to Lowestoft, Lynn, and even Grimsby, in great cultural
centres such as St Alban's Abbey, and crucially, of course,
in London and Westminster themselves. The factors that
favoured East Midland were geographical, economic and
political, and never in the first place aesthetic.

It would be easy, and not very sensible, to pick on
features of some other medieval dialect of English, and to
wish that we had for their sake adopted the whole dialect

63

instead of East Midland; but, for instance, the pretty *u* sound of West Midland and South-Western, comparable with the French *u* or German *ü*, was so little regarded by its users that it has died out even in those dialect areas—areas where some of the most attractive Middle English poetry was composed, in sounds now muted. No dialect of England was intrinsically the 'best' as a standard, whatever good features it may have had; but I could argue that medieval Scots would have made a very handy standard tongue, with Northern English in second place.

The Standard Accepted (or Received Standard) speech of the educated Londoner and Southerner has some obvious shortcomings. A combination of urban catarrh, affectation, moneyed eloquence, and a strong stress on the penultimate or antepenultimate syllables of long words, has produced a glut of syllables with the vowel *ə*, the flat neuter noise which dominates the first, third and fourth syllables of *photographer*. I do not want to impose the phonetic alphabet on printer or reader, but they must accept at least *ə*; and I hope that a frank respelling like *fətógrəfə* will alarm and humble those who have been toying with 'spelling reform' on a phonetic basis—but I must not trespass on my next chapter. No dialect uses *ə* as frequently as does the Accepted, and none so shortens and blurs the good old long vowels: whereas the North still uses the historically long forms of *tooth* and *book*, the South has for years shortened them, with the fashionable short form of *room* coming into vogue in my own lifetime. This loss of long, clear monosyllables is regrettable; with it may be considered the nasty unrounding of the short *u* in *cut* or *up* (which the North still keeps with the vowel of *put*), whereby the homely phrase *shut up!* works its way even further into bizarre forms that sound like *shattáp!* And while this good old short *oo* is becoming *ə* and then almost *a*, another kind of *a* is busily being turned by elegant speech into the *e* of *Bleckheath* or *pussyket*, and by young actors (as a correspondent to the *Radio Times* complained after a broadcast of 9 June 1974) into the first noise of *ungry* and *gumble*.

Worst of all, Cockney diphthongisation has long ago polluted the old pure long *i* and long *u* sounds (still heard in Scots renderings of, say, *bright* and *sour*) into diphthongs with *a* as their first element; yet these new versions of such words as *my* and *our* were only a beginning—the next stage achieved the loss of the second element, the *original* element, until many elegant Southerners took to saying *ma* and *ah* for these two possessives. *We're having to rebuild the top of ah spa*, I was told by a Home Counties vicar, a man of good bearing and breeding; that sounds which were once as in *bee* and *boo*, and later as in *by* and *bough*, should now occur equally as long *a*, is both curious and disappointing. Those of us who are not middle-class citizens of the capital of England are stuck at the intermediate stage, the diphthongs, and fortunately we do not have to follow the lower-class Londoners into their other shocking diphthongisation of *pay day* to *pie die* (will this one day turn into *pa da*?) or of *cocoa* into *cowcow*. A Cumbrian friend of mine, losing her way in the Lake District during World War II, asked a child the way to the tarn, but chose the wrong child, a London evacuee, and was directed to Penrith, the nearest town; and oh! there is no doubt that real Cockney, despite all its delicious associations of pluck and humour and broadmindedness, is a very ugly wrenching of distinguishable sounds into indistinguishable. All city

E   65

dialects tend to suffer from the effects of catarrh (the Cardiff snarl is sometimes called *catarrhdiff*), haste, smoking, fumes, shouting (especially against the telly), gang-speech, and protest; and some are indefensible, especially Brum and (with its *fur wur and tur*) Liverpuddlian. Southern Accepted is certainly preferable to these, but why has the English of England so utterly effaced the final *r* and even the medial one? By way of compensation, it notoriously puts in a gratuitous one in such phrases as *the idear of it*, frequently heard on the 'media'. It is chiefly in Wales and Scotland now that one hears the *r* of *better* or *forget* or *world*, and the English grow up to sound the *r* with top teeth and lower lip instead of with tongue and hard palate, though any bellicose child knows how to make machine-gun noises with the latter set of equipment.

Southerners, even when they are neither slovenly nor affected, use by training a dialect which is one of the least precise; it is strange that underprivileged slum-dwellers and overprivileged latifundists have concurred in mangling their vowels and in slurring away their consonants. Really nice people are supposed to say *gel, umour, huntin,* and (until this century) *ain't*; but then, so do some rather nasty ones. 'The people in between', saddled with a dialect that early sloughed the plural nouns in *-en* and eventually the singular verbs in *-eth*, employ this blunted instrument with more or less care, and of course really nice people never join the plebs in saying *be'er* for *better*, or *nuffin* or *corbloimey*; but it is still like their sauce to poke fun at even plebby speakers in Wales, Scotland, Yorkshire, or Devon, whose sounds would often be far more acceptable to an impartial judge of the efficacy and euphony of habits of speech. It had better be pointed out at once that Welsh,

66

contrary to standard English belief, is *not* a dialect, but a language. As for Anglo-Welsh, even its supposed features like *he do go* are from over the Border in Gloucestershire; it has clear enunciation (like *butter* with a doubled *t* and a trilled *r*), proper aspirates, and vowels that are far less often *ə*; syntax such as *Come you over by here from by there* or *It's raining pouring* is variously an invention of Stage Welsh or a translation from a different Welsh idiom. Scots is admirable: it has kept some lovely pure long vowels, the reality of consonants, and that slight slowness that helps the speaker and the listener towards better communication. But if slowness were the criterion, the South-West would seem to have great strengths; it lingers delightedly over final *-er* sounds, without ever quite reaching a proper trill, and Bristol speech has its own strange refinement, in that a final *-a* collects an *-l* by the overscrupulous habit of not leaving the tongue hanging in mid-mouth but of lightly touching the hard palate with it: it is notorious that Bristol girls are called Normal and Idal and Eval, that countries and diseases turn up in forms like Russial and malarial, that they ask you if you have any ideal of the time, and that *-ra* actually collects a little *i*-glide that adorns the name of Frank Sinatrial. Bristol admittedly has some horrible pronouns and verb forms such as ' 'Er wouldn't suit I' or 'They knows where you'm to'; on the other hand, the Bristol use of *thou/thee*, and of the verb *to be*, although corrupted into forms like *thee bist*, is nearer to the West Saxon that King Alfred spake and to the hearts of those of us who wish that *you* had stayed plural, and its past and present of *to dare not*—*dursn't* and *dassn't* (known elsewhere)—have a similar warmth and flavour.

I have loitered over Bristol speech because I live in the

67

midst of it; similar excursions could gather up other isolated glories and oddities, the former showing that every dialect has a right to a hearing—this is plain justice, anyway. Since grammar-books are only books of etiquette, and since Received Standard is only the dialect of the London middle class, we must speak of differences, not corruptions (the dialect form may well be the older-established), and of characteristics, not faults; I admit that strong dialect variations distract the reader's or listener's attention from *what* to *how*, but all of us, however well trained, speak a dialect of our own, a little idiolect nurtured in the microclimate of our upbringing, our adenoids, our reticence, our shrill nervousness, our ponderousness, our love of music, our tone-deafness, our inclination to act even when off a stage, or any other ways that we have of going about things. Some regional words are so shapely, so useful, that they deserve to be adopted officially; these include some of the French words pressed into Scots service during the Auld Alliance, such as *douce* as the adjective for a nice little lady, *bonny*, and the proud *policies* for the land, however small, around a house. And how have we managed without *lumpernscrump*, which the man at Kilve in Somerset told me his rain-soaked beet would do for?—it turned out to mean 'pig-food', and any more swillful and troughy piece of hog language could hardly be devised. Where there is a serious discrepancy between two meanings, it would be reasonable for the rare and regional to yield: the Northern *starved with cold* contains an older use than the Southern restriction of *starve* to hunger, but is now more quaint than serviceable; many must have encountered the Scots phrase *Do you mind?* and wondered how they had given the impression of being offended; a Northern lorry-driver in Bristol was genuinely delayed and (when all the horns were sounding behind him) puzzled at the dockside notice *Wait while the lights are flashing*—they weren't, but he dutifully waited *until* they were. My first awareness of difficulty over Scots was across the Border near Dumfries, when I asked a countryman where he lived: 'I stay beside my grandmother'.—'Yes, but where do you *live*?' ... Scots, like American, tends to use *this* in certain cases where Standard Accepted uses *that*; I am told that when the telephone rings in America one is liable to pick up the receiver and hear a voice saying 'Who is *this*?', as if initiating a guessing-game. The Southern Englishman rejects one Northern idiom which evokes a particularly painful memory for me, of an un-inspired art master who used to hit us cruelly across the head and who always ended our lessons by saying 'I want this finishing by Friday'; yet this strange active use (as opposed to the passive *finished*) is acceptable in flavoured old expressions such as 'I have heard tell' and 'hearsay'. Some Scots have a queer variant of it: 'My umbrella needs recovered', where an ellipsis has occurred as in their idiom 'The cat wants oot'.

Oddly, where we *have* adopted dialect forms as official, they are often either of no particular importance, such as *vat* and *vixen* with their non-East-Midland voicing of *f-* to *v-*, or rather vicious forms that supplanted something more precise and euphonious: above all, the *-s* (from Northern) that replaced *-th* in the third person singular of the present indicative. This last injudicious choice sums up, I think, the capricious way in which we have found our great norm of speech; the old U and non-U monographs, which seemed at times to record disinterestedly and at others to prescribe and proscribe with venomous humour, neither condoned nor condemned the kind of voice that produces in-bred sounds such as 'He thet heth yas to hya let him hya'.

One further point. The existence of dialects all over the English-speaking world is the greatest bulwark against 'spelling reform'; for which, as for so many other reasons, long may they flourish!

8

OUR UNPOPULAR ALPHABET: PUNCTUATION

Will it seem paradoxical on my part if I now turn from these seven chapters of pained and fretful strictures about accepted usage, and introduce our unpopular alphabet and our weird spelling system by saying that I am almost wholly content with them? I shall go on putting the term 'spelling reform' into quotation marks, because it is as hypothetical and deceptive as 'The Conifers' for a house with a dwarf larch in the garden. Briefly, the spelling of English cannot be reformed, and should not be even if it could; a phonetic alphabet is out of the question for English. There is a two-fold objection, of time and place, even without our calling on the centuried traditions that have composed our spelling. The objection relating to time is slight, and would not by itself be insuperable: that a phonetic spelling stabilised in the year x would not be representative of all the habits of speech in the year $x + 50$, the reason being that little changes and vogues tend to set in; yet it would still be fairly accurate, utterly so in most words, and adjustable in the few new forms. In the times of Swift and Byron, a vase was probably a *vais*, in my childhood it was in many areas a *vawze*, it has now changed firmly to a *varze*, and in America it is a *vaize*; but this is an extreme case, and champions of phonetic spelling might even argue that the spelling would impose a stabilised pronunciation that would last as long as the script was understood.

The objection relating to place is, however, unanswerable. To succeed, any reform would have to be universal; it is not just that all printers and publishers would have to adopt the new system (a comparatively tiny difficulty), or that the public would have to talk classlessly (though I cannot think that this would be enthusiastically adopted), but that the system would have to apply to all English-speaking areas. By whatever means could this be imposed? Yorkshiremen found the early Pitman shorthand difficult because it was based on assumptions of sound different from theirs; and it is absurd to suppose that people who have always called a calf a 'caff' or a 'cawf' will stop doing so when a new spelling tells them that it should be 'carf'— whereas they are quite happy to acknowledge the justice of the four letters, including the silent *l*, and of what they 'mean' when juxtaposed. A 'reader' who reads letter by letter, and not in whole words and so in phrases and sentences, is hardly an adult reader at all, and the vagaries of our spelling do not impose the difficulties which the 're-formers' claim; indeed, foreigners will tell us that the irregularity proved often to be a real mnemonic, and children learning Latin found *iter itineris* and *fero ferre tuli latum* much easier to fix in their minds than the just slightly messy antics of *civis* and *rego*. Yet for the pedantic principle of one-letter-one-sound the 'reformer' would alienate all the millions who speak English in the five continents, including the Welsh, the Scots, and most Englishmen;

72

instead of being united by the spelling of our wonderful language, a spelling which they can and do interpret as they please, they would find that the new orthography dictated—as if they were colonists dependent on the cream of the Home Counties—a pronunciation which is largely alien to them.

In a way, I should end my treatment of 'spelling reform' here. Certainly it would be wrong to cite the material and commercial objections of new type, new methods for schools, the vast cost of reprinting everything, and the obsolescence of the British Museum Library and all others; if the 'reform' was salutary, even these expensive changes could and should be undertaken. Even the difficulty of re-learning should not be stressed, although a British newspaper early in 1960 carried a stern warning about spelling from a thrice-in-a-lifetime reformed Norwegian. All that matters is that millions of people all over the world, at present applying our spelling to their own idiolects, would with 'spelling reform' suffer the imposition of a system welcome to a tiny minority of them. And they would surely shun it, and go their own idiosyncratic ways; the break-up of Latin around the Mediterranean into French, Italian, Spanish, Portuguese, Provençal, Roumanian, Romansh, and smaller units, would have nothing on the universal dismemberment of English.

But I must go further, because various national academies and congresses have used their good influence to promote stable phonetic spelling which has presumably been reinterpreted by dialect speakers and yet has the apparent merit of consistency within itself; so why cannot English be treated in the same way?—and why should uniformly well educated Londoners not be enabled to use the same convention for *off* as for *trough*? (whatever they may want to do with these in Auckland or Anchorage). Such questions must be answered, and easily can be; English is not in this being proud, traditionalist, reactionary, and my first reason for saying so is historical.

A language cannot, by Act of Parliament, or plebiscite, or evolution, completely disengage itself from its history, and the history of English is more complicated than that of any other because of that 'layering' of three language stocks with which I started Chapter 2. Even counting only the first two, Germanic and Romance, we shall find that their methods of spelling are very different, so which method should be paramount?—*fish* or *fission*, *news* or *fuse*, *kernel* or *colonel* (one of which must honestly be lost)? Under the terms of 'reform', it would obviously be abominable to let *fish* and *physics* exist side by side; but even if those of us who shrink from beginning *physics* with an *f* were reminded that the lordly language of Castile is not ashamed to write *física* for it, we could still reply that this is much less bizarre than the *fiziks* which scrupulousness would impose upon us. Here, of course, is another potential horror: our language would grow further away from the languages which it has so happily plundered. What good Frenchman would recognise *kwoliti* (for *q*, like the *c* in *physics*, must be one of the letters doomed to the chop) or *sentə*?—what good Frisian would acknowledge two words that he shares with us, *butə* and *tshiiz* (or however we must show long *ee*)? I know that English spelling was not devised, or allowed to develop, for the sake of foreigners learning the language; but 'spelling reform' would certainly make their task far harder.

Not only would the links with tributary languages be

74

severed, but relations within our own vocabulary would cease to be recognisable: *woman* would look nothing like *women*; the Romance *revise* and *revision* would go separate ways with their new *aiz* and *izh*, as would *benign* and *benignant*; *two* would seem unrelated to *twice*, and the new *wun* would stand aloof from *only* and further than before from its cognates *an*, *union*, and *onion*; *England* would acquire an initial *I* which the Scots, naturally less touchy in the matter, already allow in their surname *Inglis*. And let us consider another aspect of *two*: it is often complained that it, and *to*, and *too*, 'all sound the same' but are spelt differently; the fact, of course, is that they don't sound the same at all, having differences of length and stress according to context, and that *to* is three words at least—the *tə* of *to London*, the *tuw* of *to Edinburgh*, and the *tuu* (or however we must show long *u*) of *to*, *not from*. But *to*, *two*, *too*, covering all the different intonations which the context imposes on them, will at once sort themselves out for the intelligent reader, and be an aid to understanding for the less intelligent. Nor is English quite alone in the tenacity of such old forms of spelling; French, Gaelic, and Modern Greek, for instance, would be far more difficult if spelt phonetically, through the falling together of so many sounds into identical spellings, of the type of our *rain*, *rein*, and *reign*, where 'reform' would leave us with one word for the price of three.

The methods suggested for 'reform' need hardly be mentioned now; even if I listed them, they could be quickly dismissed. The 'reform' movement has been the pastime of amateurs, the hobby-horse of certain printers, and the cynical fling of Bernard Shaw, who left it his money—over which more dabblers were soon busy competing. Benjamin Franklin, in his *Philosophical Miscellanies* (1779), pooh-poohed the objections, beginning with the loss of etymologies; he was right in this particular, since a dictionary would be able to track the origin down for us, and since in any case words suffer so many changes of their primeval meaning, but he was deaf, in his cleverness and superiority, to the sounds made by all but the élite, and he tacitly assumed that all would conform to the standard sound as soon as they caught sight of the standard spelling. Noah Webster, agreeing with him that 'a reformation of our orthography' was 'practicable and highly necessary', shows by his preference for the pronunciations *clerk* (with a real *e*), *quality* (with a real *a*), *eether*, *erb*, *deef*, *nature* (with a real *t*, not a *tsh*), and others, how easily the spelling of English and American English might have bifurcated if he had had his way. As it is, the few divergences of American spelling are so slight and futile that they might just as well be normalised to the insular version again: *color* and *center* are intrinsically no better than *colour* and *centre* at representing a word that ends in *ə*, *program* and *catalog* (why not *drum-majoret*?) merely save letters and call up dull and misleading analogies with rams and logs, *traveler* tempts to a pronunciation *travéeler*, and *esthetic* is unhelpfully further from the original Greek; these tinkerings with spelling seem to me merely divisive.

In Britain, the many suggestions for a new alphabet have included the sloughing of the redundant letters *c*, *j* (what, make it *dzh*?), *q*, *x*—though *f* is a luxury for *ph* (in view of the necessity for *th*) and *v* for *bh*. Or these six could be retained and reused; let us imagine *x* as standing for *ə*, and then *photographer* could be spelt *fxtógrxfx*. Silent *e* would have to go—but, strangely, this would create extra forms to learn, since where we now happily use *stranded*, *stilled* and *stopped*, we should have to write the last two as *stild/stilld* and *stopt*; and once the final silent *e* of *mate*, *mete*, *mite*, *mote*, *mute*, was truly put to silence, how should we show long vowels?—by doubling them, or (as some experts have urged) by diacritics? Now English has up to this point mercifully escaped macrons and cedillas and circumflexes and tildes and the rest, save for loan-words such as *Nō-play* and *façade* and *rôle*, and I propose that we take every means to go on avoiding them. The much ridiculed *wr* and *gh* would have to be stifled, of course, with the very proper result that *right*, *rite*, *wright*, and *write*, would all look the same: to whose advantage? The final extermination of the mute letters in *mb*, *ps*, *pt*, *pn*, *gn*, *kn*, would add its toll of problems—first, with the falling together of such words as *new*, *gnu* and *knew*, and secondly, in the profitless escape from, especially, Greek originals. The letter *z* would come into its own, as Chapter 4 made clear, and would give us two forms for the plural noun (*pots*, but *panz*), the genitive singular and plural of the noun (*bishop's/bishops'*, *dean'z/deanz'*), and the third person singular present indicative (*subtracts*, *addz*); I suppose we might get used to it.

The most determined scheme for 'reform', and the one officially favoured, subsidised, and hustled into experimental use in schools, is the Initial Teaching Alphabet; I first heard of it at Oldham, where the decent little Lancastrians were presumably being taught that *u* exemplified in *up* was the flat Southern version, and not the rich *put* sound of their legitimate speech. It was intended for beginners, to give them confidence; after about eighteen months they were to transfer to traditional spelling. Newspapers have brimmed with correspondence (not often written in ITA) about its merits and failings; not having myself used it, or had speech with any of its guineapigs, I can only look coolly at it and detect its many anomalies. Thus *a* of 'apple' and *u* of 'up' are ligatured into another letter; an intelligent and quick-eared child will discern at once that this must say something like the *ou* of *out*, but no! —it is the sound in 'author'. There is a ligature of the old 'long *s*' and *h* for 'ship', but a special luxurious sign of its own for the 'trea*s*ure' sound—why not a *zh* ligature? And if the *sh* ligature is meaningful, then the fancy *c* + *h* ligature should be *tsh*. Since *y* ('yellow') and an *oo* symbol exist, why a *u* + *e* ligature for 'due' and (though it isn't mentioned) 'dew'?—such favouritism is contrary to all phonetic principles. Further, the suggested *c* of 'cat' and the *k* of 'kitten' are as much the same letter as the *t* of 'tree' and the *phth* of 'phthisis'—why make exceptions, and who chooses when the *c* or *k* is to be used? The reversed *z* of 'is' and the *z* of 'zoo' are likewise the same letter. Why *wh* ligatured, if we are to be systematically helpful?— clearly, *hw* is the only reasonable way of showing this double sound, as the Anglo-Saxons demonstrated long ago. Two different fancy *t* shapes are ligatured with *h* for the 'three' and 'mother' sounds; but surely *dh* makes better sense for the second? If anyone tells me that *dh* is not a native habit, I can give the sensible answer that any symbol would suffice (especially an informative one like this, which shows the voiced *d* quality), if the thing is to be forgotten after a year and a half. Worst of all, I can't find how to spell *murder*; neither of the vowels has a place in the alphabet—perhaps the tots are being protected from the word.

Now very much of what I said at the outset of this chapter was powerfully treated by Sir William Craigie in the 59th and 63rd tracts of the Society for Pure English, *Some Anomalies of Spelling* (1942) and *Problems of Spelling Reform* (1944); he showed more forbearance than I have chosen to show, but his scholarship built up against 'reform' an indestructible case which he had already inaugurated in his book *English Spelling, Its Rules and Reasons* (1927). But, as if out of courtesy, he appears to stay his hand from using to the full one of the most powerful weapons in his armoury: ə.

As soon as we involve this most popular of our vowels in any scheme of 'reform', we see convincingly the crucial reason why a phonetic spelling system is doomed. Let us again consider the word *photograph*: boldly casting aside its history, as enshrined in the Greek stems *phot-* and *graph-*, and using a very homely phonetic system, we give it a new, true shape as (say) *fóotəgráaf*—long vowels doubled, acute accents on stressed syllables; foolproof and perfect. So a man who *makes* the things, the 'agent' in *-er*, is obviously a *fóotəgráafə*?—well, no: he is a *fətógrəfə*. Perhaps the adjective will be closer?—it is *fóotəgráfik*, with the slight worry that the long *o* isn't as long as it was in the head-word, and that it certainly bears a lighter stress. The hideous word *fətógrəfə* should, in fact, be two words, because a good speaker would make it *fətógrəfər* before a following vowel such as the *i* in *is*. That words in such intimate relationship with one another should be so sundered by their spelling is unconscionable; that the historic vowels should so often be shown as ə must lead to confusion and give no help with meanings. A sound phonetic spelling, enclosed in square brackets after a word in a foreign beginner's

79

handbook, is a good idea, but as a means of mediating English it would be merely droll.

Having thus expressed my satisfaction at our present spelling, I must continue in this encomiastic mood and make reference to our punctuation, which is simple and sound. The Spanish habit of preceding questions and exclamations with reversed question marks and exclamation marks, so as to get the voice ready, might be profitably introduced, but our system as it stands will suffice. Two very wrong things are being done with it, however. One concerns the division of two sentences by a comma; this belongs to postcard style ('We are having fabulous weather, the hotel is fantastic'), but in responsible writing it should be remembered that two sentences bearing on the same subject should be demarcated by a semi-colon (or, with discretion, a dash), and that two that are less interdependent need a full stop, which some call a full point, between them. My other warning also concerns the comma: a comma must be inserted before an adjectival clause that *describes*, and a comma must not be inserted before an adjectival clause that *defines*; thus 'my wife whom I met in Bognor' suggests that there are other wives met elsewhere, and 'my son, who is at college' is correct only if there are no other sons. Schools, I believe, still warn their pupils against brackets, dashes, and underlinings; they won't like this book at all, but these three marks are aids to full expressiveness, and warnings might well be superseded by encouragements to use the comma freely and sensibly as a pause-stop for the reader, so that he can hear in his mind's ear and receive the flow and emphasis and 'sense' at once. For really bad punctuation there is no excuse save fear.

9

OUR MISUSE OF OUR HERITAGE: THE MISPLACED WORD

We reach here the hinge of this book. Up to this point I have been dealing with the linguistic hurts and wrenchings and decays which we have inherited, and the milder adventures of the language, and its little pockets of conservatism; no single generation, for instance, is to blame for our auxiliary verbs, and we cannot hope to amend them quickly, but must simply make the best of the system that we are stuck with. But from now on I must castigate our abuse of the heritage; when perfectly clear and handsome idioms are available, and we render them obscure and ugly, only we are blameworthy.

Until recently, misuse came from ignorance and from lack of training; good speech was not disliked for its goodness, though of course high-falutin words and a la-di-da accent were the objects of plebeian scorn if their practitioners were mincing or fastidious or snobbish or arrogant or witless. The poor and uneducated would have liked to speak better; it was a means to a better job, and rough parents conscientiously paid to put their children to 'elocution' lessons, which must have achieved some little where the home circumstances were favourable. It was possible for an academic to travel in a train with labouring men, especially in Wales and Scotland, and to have a shared conversation where his standards of speech were a challenge that was accepted; in England, perhaps, there was more often a harmless suspicion of correct speech and of book-learning, and a not unreasonable defence of demotic expression, but any man would in a while respond to an English that was simple, logical, lively, and clearly enunciated.

But in a letter to *The Times* of 4 July 1973, a grammar school headmaster wrote: 'In the present craving for equality it is regarded by many of the young as élitist to use the Queen's English with discrimination, and paternalistic to express concern.' If this is true, then the danger to the language is very great; that literary and colloquial English may occupy different levels and, though of equal merit, may have different standards and techniques, has long seemed unavoidable, but that they should be in opposed political and social camps is a disaster. I am not counting here as literary English the typical sex-and-violence stuff of the railway station bookstalls, which merely enacts the fantasies of the worst of the young (and the senile); the speech of these louts, when it is audible, is gross without realism, audacious without picturesqueness, irreverent without humour, and deep in those troughs of ambiguity and cacophony which I have pleaded against throughout. Probably their foolish attitude is not worth considering here, and may prove to be transitory, but while it lasts we can feel astonishment that a whole group of society should seek to degrade their language by deliberately speaking in a way that will be less cogent, less clear, less interesting, than the means available and known to them. Even if there is some excuse in their rejection of the speech of the élite, in that they see the élite not doing their duty, not setting a standard, using place and privilege, and speaking with the evasiveness of politicians—even so, their thesis is profoundly wrong: the financial élite, the 'swells' of a former day, do not always speak an acceptably Standard English at all, but can mutilate their vowels and produce their *gel* and *huntin* to the confusion of lesser mortals. The old U *versus* non-U controversy revealed that really 'nice' speech was largely a matter of calling things by their right names, which—rather surprisingly—were usually simpler and more basic than the terms used by the bourgeoisie: *sick* at sea, not *ill*; *napkin*, not *serviette*; *suit*, not *costume*; anything rather than *toilet*. Some words, of course, were not to be used at all, *fish-knife* being just a chimera in any decent household; *dinner* didn't occur at midday, with the painful choice of *lunch* or *luncheon* to complicate matters. The important point was to avoid being genteel, and here at least Dives and the oaf are in full agreement. But good, honest people, whatever their status by birth or attainment, can and often do speak a good, honest English which it is my delight to defend.

Let me turn firmly now to those who are willing, and even eager, to speak and write effectively and, at best, eloquently. I want to set down inexorably the principal errors that I see and hear in the English of today, errors that depend not on the shortcomings of our language but on the present abuse of it; though the first, in fact, does arise from what I have said in criticism of our grammatical

83

machinery. I mean the word or phrase that dangles between two or more possible references.

When I was a schoolboy, a lot of useful fun was made of the dangling participle, and the first I can remember was well designed to amuse: 'Did you see the grandfather's clock coming upstairs?' For my part, I think that I would never have said that; but, allowing it to be possible, we see that the word-order would be harmless in a richly inflected language—*coming* would be nominative singular (masculine or feminine), and no ridiculous interpretation would occur to anyone. But, as I made clear at the end of Chapter 3, we cannot disarray our words in a language so lightly inflected as English; we cannot assume that the juxtaposed *clock* and *coming* will be dissociated by a sudden onset of commonsense. What is further surprising, however, in the repeated warnings against the dangling participle is that the participle gets all the blame: the dangling word, or phrase, includes it, and has a far wider currency and scope.

Danger looms in even the innocuous-looking idiom: a friend of mine, hearing that an aged jeweller was critically ill, called at his Bristol shop, asked the girl assistant 'Could you tell me how old Mr Kemp is?', and received the answer 'Oh, about eighty-five, I think'. There is no folly in his phrasing or in her answer, but it is a striking example of how wrong meanings may be imposed on words when their syntactical relationship is not grammatically fixed. In looser sentences, however, there is less excuse for disarray; a 1972 essay, written for me on *Troilus and Criseyde*, attempted one effect, but produced another, in the sentence 'Grey day dawns as the lovers lie in bed almost like an omen'. A caption to a photograph in

84

the *Illustrated London News* in 1964 entangled a straight-forward scene with the words 'The Bride and Bridegroom leave, the Bride wearing a 20-foot train and the bridal veil worn by her mother and grandmother'; all right, only a fool would see anything bizarre in this, but formally *veil worn* can be a construction parallel with *Bride wearing*, and not just a hypothetical 'accusative' as object of *wearing*. The old dialogue 'I want to have my children young'/ 'Yes, it seems silly to have old children' shows up the penury of our grammar and warns us against the false economy of ellipsis and of omitting useful little connectives.

An added ambiguity occurs when a word can be either of two parts of speech; the Rugby League television commentator who said 'We've seen Widnes making a come-back before this season' was forgetting (pardonably, in the heat of following a fast game) that *before* is a preposition as well as an adverb. If the preposition is meant, then the phrase is easily placed as 'Before this season, we've . . .'; if the adverb, then the sentence could end '. . . this season before'. Or something is suppressed by ellipsis, but its indignant shade haunts the vestigial sentence; hence the man complaining of the price of beef, who said 'I eat more than two chickens every week'—which is hardly worth mentioning if the verb *eat* or *do* is 'understood' after *chickens*. A more damaging economy, involving also the bad use of *terrible* in relation to weather, enlivened the *Llandaff* (Cathedral) *Monthly* for July 1972: 'Our thanks are due to Mr and Mrs Duncan Alexander for their hospitality on such a terrible evening'; Mr and Mrs Alexander will readily forgive me for quoting this—the real and happy meaning is obvious, but the bad weather should ideally have been given a sentence or clause on its

85

own, before the pleasant outcome of the evening was stated. Similarly, in the University of Bristol *Alumni Gazette* for 1974, a talk 'was attended by over 100 people, about half of whom had enjoyed an informal buffet supper'; what had been the reaction of the other half? All I can say of another ill assembled (and probably apocryphal) magazine jotting—'Miss X is leaving the parish; she is one of those to whom we are sorry to say Au Revoir but not Goodbye'—is that it is seriously wrong.

Our newspapers bristle with phrases which have wandered inside their sentences, or which are not as they stand acceptable without some amplification. Said a *Western Mail* headline in 1964, 'Son "run in" for theft by father'; they coyly put *run in* into quotation marks, as if in apology for being so slangy, but they would have spent their time better in making it clear whether the father did the running-in or the thieving. The *South Wales Echo* in 1974 said that 'A nationwide file is being kept on "amorous patients" who send their doctors love gifts and letters to help protect the doctors from misconduct allegations'— where a comma after *letters* would have helped substantially, and a complete rearrangement even more so. An eminent *Daily Express* example deserves an exact reference —2 March 1963: at a Coventry factory 'The strikers allege that the management attempted to time women using the lavatory as part of a productivity campaign'. And even *The Times* (albeit in the Personal Column, 1964) allowed 'Sir Gerald Kelly wishes to trace a painting of a life-size nude girl by the late Sir George Clausen called *Primavera* . . .'; I *think* that a life-size painting was wanted —most girls are life-size. As I have said before, it is only fair and right to be gentle with newspaper headlines, since they must do their task so briefly; yet it is not the brevity, but the order, that vitiates the *Bristol Evening Post*'s 1959 announcement 'Tried to Kill Himself Twice, Court Told', where 'Twice Tried . . .' would avoid any suggestion of the impossible. Every potted and capitalised clause or phrase like 'Man Kicked in Window' poses the question *Did he?* or *Was he?*—is *kicked* an active past tense or a passive past participle, is *in* an adverb or a preposition? And remember again, as we saw in another context in Chapter 3: every adjective + two compounded nouns, and every adjective + noun in the possessive + noun, is misplaced by reason of its ambiguity; what, unequivocally, is *Temporary Signalling Difficulty?*—or a *Unique Gentleman's Residence?* —or a *17-year-old baby's nanny?*—or a *neglected servants' entrance?*

One of the words that dangles to worst purpose is *because* after a negative statement. Let the reader consider frankly whether the following sentence irritates him: 'I'm not going out for a walk because it's raining.' At once, of course, in writing, we can adjust it by a firm comma after *walk*, though many writers would leave this to chance; but in speech a quite sensible wrong meaning lurks—'I'm going out for a walk—not because it's raining' (after all, plenty of gusty people like walking in the rain); the re-arrangement: 'Because it's raining, I'm not going out for a walk' is the straight solution.

Well, the written sentence needed only a comma, and I perhaps seem to be fussing over very little. But observe how easily this particular ambiguity can develop; a seriously meant hymn, translated from a majestic Spanish sonnet of the Renaissance period, begins

My God, I love Thee, not because
I hope to gain thereby.

Does he so hope or *not* hope?—it would be Christian to
discount any gain, to regard his future gain as irrelevant
or even unlikely. If you reply that *of course* he hopes, and
that this is made perfectly obvious, then I shall present you
with the statement 'I'm going to forgive you, not because
you deserve forgiveness', where the opposite meaning,
expressed by the same formula, is equally obvious. No
language should tolerate this state of affairs; yet listen to a
good stylist, and a good commentator on language, falling
with commotion into the trap: Rebecca West, in the
Sunday Telegraph of 30 April 1972, wrote that 'This is unlikely, not because the English are incapable of cruelty (as
Cromwell showed) but because they have very bad
memories'; so are the English incapable of cruelty or not,
and did Cromwell show them to be incapable of cruelty or
not? Worse, because more elaborate and indeed tortuous,
is on page 496 of Fowler's *Modern English Usage*, revised by
Sir Ernest Gowers—this from prescriptive grammarians!
'*Previous to* and *Prior to* are grammatically blameless, but
that does not justify their use as substitutes for *before* because they are thought to be grander or more genteel';
even if we grant that the omission of any comma before
the word *because* almost clinches the right meaning, there
are other interpretations floating around, too. *Because* in
all such sentences is no more dangerous than *since* or *as*;
in fact, I prefer to avoid these two when I mean *because*—
the connotations of time in the one, and of likeness in the
other, give them enough work to do elsewhere. But we can
take this prefaced negative further; the ambiguity of

putting a purpose clause or phrase after it is well seen in the genuine (so they say) statement by a parson: 'I wear no clothes to distinguish me from my parishioners.'

So we can reach the misplaced *only*. I see that Simeon Potter, in *Our Language* (pages 100–1), doesn't mind this, and that Fowler-Gowers rather heavy-handedly maintain that a lot too much stir is made about it. To me, it remains nastily and obviously and avoidably wrong. To say 'He only died a week ago' is, despite their defence of it, to suggest that all sorts of things more important could have happened to him; the rule is simple—that *only* stands immediately before the word or phrase that it modifies.

10

THE FOUR WICKEDEST IDIOMS

I want to devote the main of this chapter to four usages which have spread, perhaps from journalese, into common and even elegant speech and writing, and which remain unpardonable when literate people use them; I may be criticised for my heavy hand laid upon them, but the case against them must be heard, and I can best begin with the improper *if*.

Students of Latin find the conditional sentences hard going; English conditionals are intrinsically very easy, but they have been affected by three horrible *if*s that poach on their preserves. *If* should preface the protasis, the condition, on which the apodosis, the statement, depends; what place has it, therefore, in such an expression as 'If the weather has been fine this August, there were far sunnier Augusts recorded in the late nineteenth century'? The only sensible formula for this remark is: Statement/comma (or semi-colon)/*but*/statement; the second half in no way at all rests on the truth of the first. Worse is the *if* of such a sentence as 'They are holding a barbecue, if you know what *that* is'; the correct counter to this would be 'They're holding one even if I *don't* know what it is', but the idiom has a crumb of excuse inasmuch as the *if*-clause is a kind of ellipsis for 'I don't know whether you know . . .'. But arising from the first kind is an even worse *if* which is gaining currency: the *if* that really stands for *although* or *although perhaps*, but stands for it very inadequately. I was astonished to see recently, in an authoritative book of reference, that Byron's relationship with his half-sister Augusta, 'if unnatural, was genuine and lasting'; what?— there was genuine fidelity only provided that the association was unnatural? In the same book, William Watson was credited with 'a true if slender talent'—so if the writer is misinformed, and the talent is considerable, then it ceases to be a real talent. Some will say that my objection is pedantry, that *if, even if, even though, though*, now shade into one another; but the simple way to express that first statement is to establish that the second part does not depend on the first but is parallel to it: the relationship 'was perhaps unnatural, but was genuine and lasting'.

And now, the improper *while*. For some years, the rumour has been spreading that *while* is a superior way of saying *and, but, whereas, though*, or a semi-colon; hence the classic 'The Bishop preached the sermon while the Dean read the lesson'. I take it that *while* should be used to show concurrence of events, and for no other purpose save in the North, where *while* is entitled to the sense 'until'. I need say no more about this plain misuse, except to add that some people think that *whilst* is even nicer, though *whilst* (from *whiles*) was once a form as slovenly as 'I seen him onst' or 'I never had a chanst', which—like *amidst* and *amongst*—add a parasitic *t* to a final *s* sound.

My third butt is the improper *was to*. Now *was to* has a real meaning: that something was meant/intended/ arranged/ordered/ordained/obliged/predestined to happen. It has no place in sentences such as these, from recent companions to, and histories of, literature—the kind of book, I admit, in which entries must sometimes be crammed into a potted formula: Mrs Humphry Ward began her career as an author, 'in the course of which she was to produce 28 novels' ('That's my lucky number, so I'll down my pen when I've written exactly twenty-eight'); Thackeray 'met and married . . . Isabella Shawe, who was to be the prototype of so many of his . . . heroines'— as if it was all calculated and convenient; *Little Dorrit* 'was to be completed in 1858'—in fact, there was no such time limit set; Mark Twain 'was to become to America what Dickens was to England'—this has an extra ugliness, the second *was to* in a different sense. With this spurious future-in-the-past goes the bogus purpose clause introduced by *to* plus an infinitive, where no such purpose could possibly be intended, and where only another *finite* verb in the same tense could be correct. Television commentator: 'They scored a penalty only to have it disallowed' (well, that was very sporting of them). *Western Daily Press* (1972): 'The driver . . . stopped and looked out of his window only to be grabbed by the hair' (*only*?—no other motive at all?). Public orator (presenting a former fire service officer for an honorary degree): '. . . returning from a scarred Birmingham to witness the first big fire raid here . . .' ('Do hurry, taxi-driver; I don't want to miss seeing a moment of those incendiary bombs'; and, incidentally, was there then an *un*scarred Birmingham, too?). A student's essay let Troilus 'sally out to battle again, to be unexpectedly killed by Achilles'; can one really plan to make the unexpected happen? Let us leave this topic with the heroic gesture of 'He left the land-rover only to be struck by a poisoned dart'.

The worst used of all words is *literally*. This means 'to the letter', in absolute truth, without any touch of metaphor or other figure; and it is now used (more often, I suspect) to mean 'figuratively', 'in a *literary* figure'. We have all heard and read such solecisms as 'I was literally petrified', 'I was literally decimated', 'I was literally flayed'—statements from which the real horror has receded. Not long ago a restive football manager was 'literally crucified'; has the fool who wrote *that* any idea of what Christ suffered on the Cross?—and could Christians and gentlemanly non-Christians please consider never using the verb *crucify* thus, even in figure? The silliest authentic example that I know was reported to me as occurring on a stationary 'bus in Clifton, Bristol, when one young man with a cultured voice said to another 'Of course, I was literally sitting on a volcano from all directions'.

Well, among individual abuses these four seem to me the worst. It is strange that grammarians and teachers have bothered so much about the split infinitive; it is neither really ugly nor really ambiguous, and it rolls off the tongue more aptly than the 'correct' form. Jane Austen split them right and left, and no one is going to criticise my Jane's style unrebuked! The fact is that *to just go* is a new and subtle infinitive form, integrated in a way that *just to go* isn't. Similarly, I have already regretted the ink spilt over the postfixed preposition, a word which is perfectly clear and which can even impart a dying fall to the cadence which the sentence ends with; whereas, in common with other civilised languages, our use of prepositions is so loose and imprecise that 'the gift of my mother-in-law' and 'the gift of a lawnmower' can refer to the same thing, and 'a broth of a boy' can contrive to have

93

a meaning. As for *like* in its frequent misuse where *as* should stand, *Modern English Usage* lays down firm rules and gives excellent examples, and I need not try to better it; it is clear that *like* is not a conjunction (so 'Do like I do' is incorrect), but a curious adjective/adverb which can behave as a preposition in 'governing' nouns. So even in a barbarous sentence such as 'Like you, I like a place like Bude' only the first *like* is formally incorrect; but the slightest extension of the third *like* leads to error—'There are good sands there, like Bude'. Fowler and Gowers do not mention, however, the common and dangerous idiom 'I feel like'; it might be better to conquer it altogether, because neither 'I feel like a wet rag' nor 'I feel like a good meal' has any real right to its meaning. The first is perhaps an extension of such statements as 'It feels like gossamer', but not a legitimate one, the new suggestion *not* being that I feel to another's touch as does a wet rag, and the Middle English version, had it lasted, would have given the more satisfactory form 'I fare as a wet rag'; the idea would be better expressed as 'I am like a wet rag', just as a man at Haccombe in Devon recently described to me his state, his predicament, his reaction, as 'I was like a nanny who's lost her pram', where his behaviour mattered rather than his 'feelings'. The second type of idiom is just slovenly, and has deserved the many facetious responses as in 'I feel like a meringue'./'You look like one, too'.

There are, as only some of us notice, many modern habits of speech which are so obviously incorrect, and so far from any hope of redemption, that I cannot choose to deal with them; their supporters will probably maintain that I am in the wrong, not they. Such are 'between you and I' (*I* is favoured as a form more elegant than *me*, apparently) and that reported snatch of student conversation: 'Janet was there'./'Janet whom?' (*whom*, as more difficult and more correct, so often, than *who*, is assumed to be a better form to use, whatever its grammatical function). From America has spread the use of *hopefully* to mean 'so I hope'; this, being ambiguous, must be put down.

It could be argued that we misplace many of our adjectives. When we say 'My second wife' we *define* her adequately; when we say 'My Greek wife' we apparently *describe* her, but there is nothing in the syntax to stop anyone from taking this epithet as defining, and thus it could suggest that one had also wives of other nationalities. Perhaps we should express it by using a clause, with a comma carefully inserted: 'My wife, who is Greek'; but it is doubtless too late to hope for so scrupulous a rule. Journalists have another habit with adjectives, that of thrusting them in unheralded; so has the man on the television who goes on about soccer and begins sentences with phrases like 'Goal-hungry Wolves . . .', but this idiom, and telescopings such as 'Portly beaming 45-year-old extrovert stockbroker Stuntney, interviewed at his Sèvres-stuffed Thames-side avant-garde bachelor villa, commented genially . . .', do at least pack abundant information into their graceless forms. Nor is this an affected vocabulary; the piling-up of literal truths is distasteful, but less so than the gentle dropping of the wrong word: a Bristol estate agent was advertising 'a very above average property', a television golf commentator said that two balls were 'both equidistant', and a packet label promised 'ten battered fishfingers'; a letter in the *Bristol Evening Post* in 1972 was from 'a shop steward, a militant to boot, and proud of it'—infelicitous phrasing in the days of kicked policemen, and oh! so emptily archaic. I am not condemning affectation outright; the highly artificial styles and idiosyncratic vocabularies of Lyly, Carlyle, 'Corvo', Firbank, and many later writers, have not only the charm of surprise but the power of the *mot juste*, whereas expressing the platitudinous simplex by the complex is insipid. One of the first casualties in the search for affectation is the verb *to be*: opposing the idea that men wear beards out of another kind of affectation, someone sensibly wrote 'Surely the affectation is in the removal of facial hair, not in its retention'; few writers would leave it at that—*is in* would be varied to *is found in, rests in, dwells in, lies in, stands in, shows in, stems from, issues from, proceeds from, belongs to, originates in, is discernible in, is ascribable to, is symptomatised by,* and thus the value of the good old plain word *is* is further cheapened.

ABSTRACTION: NOUNINESS: PASSIVITY: NEGATIVITY

The reluctance to say *is* when you mean *is*, with which I closed the last chapter, is often only part of a larger hesitancy, of an attitude of mind that casts over the plain and certain a veil of the vague and provisional. Or, to put it more bluntly, there are writers so gingerly and yet so pretentious that they turn statements about real objects and real actions into elaborate and inappropriate webs of abstraction. Or, to put it more formally, some writers prefer abstract nouns and depersonalised verbs to all other kinds of expression, whatever the subject. Or, to put it more tolerantly, some writers, or speakers, treat the creative act of writing, or speaking, with such respect that they give even the simplest statement the framework of a period sentence in which long and searching words, often in pairs that are nearly doublets, are articulated by little auxiliary verbs; the statement is not so much related as that light is shed on it by reference to its implications, its spirit, its essence; its original simplicity is assumed and dismissed—now a worthwhile interpretation is offered.

Such sentencing can be very agreeable. Carlyle, writing of the start of Louis XVI's reign in *The French Revolution*, conveys the coming horrid deeds almost entirely in abstractions:

> There is a stillness, not of unobstructed growth, but of passive inertness, the symptom of imminent downfall. As victory is silent, so is defeat. Of the opposing forces the weaker has resigned itself; the stronger marches on, noiseless now, but rapid, inevitable: the fall and overturn will not be noiseless.

Here the only two verbs (apart from *to be*) are *resign* and *march*, and both are used metaphorically; yet things are happening, with more vividness and vibrancy than if the normal interactions of real verbs and concrete nouns had been allowed. To use a briefer piece of abstraction: when Frederick William 'Serafino Austin Lewis Mary' Rolfe, self-styled Baron Corvo, wrote in *Hubert's Arthur* that 'There was a great crown-wearing this day in King William Redhair his hall at Westminster', he achieved, in his best perverse manner, a variety of effects good and bad; using *his* for *'s* is ignorant and unhistorical (though better men than Corvo had been misled into it), and refusing to call William II *Rufus* or today *today* imparts some odd flavour that could be found attractive, but the solemn abstraction *crown-wearing* sums up the awe of the situation far better than would a concrete statement such as 'The king was officially wearing his crown'. Wordsworth commemorated his little dead daughter in a sonnet which is both pathetic and accurate—he instinctively turns to share a pleasant impression with her, and then remembers that she is no longer with him; in so simple a setting, we can feel no distaste at the ponderous polysyllable chosen

98

to give its abstract force to her tomb, 'That spot which no vicissitude can find'.

Then, too, if a subject is of great philosophical depth, and treats of theory or speculation or the emotions or religion or logic or almost any of the -isms, it is likely to be best mediated by the international learnèd vocabulary of long Latinate words. We may well feel that a designedly rough native word like *thisness*, however effective in isolation, looks more out of place among its normal philosophical fellows than would *haecceity*; and we may easily be embarrassed by G. M. Hopkins's *inscape* and *instress*. We should not expect to find fresh beauty or sensual word-pictures or exciting flesh-and-blood colours in the language of grave theory, and there is a whole unattractive word, *concretism*, for the practice of regarding as concrete that which is abstract; this sounds to me a livelier practice than its converse, but still a wrong one. On the other hand, great minds—the tellers of parables, the teachers and interpreters of their generations—have found it practicable to exhibit their truths either straight and then in homely narrative form, or the other way round, or by narrative alone. This is the stuff of allegory, of the sudden sweet madness of metaphor, of Aesop, of *De profundis*, and of the burning, curative 'poultice of penance' in a medieval lyric; but equally attractive to many fine minds is the cool detachment, a detachment almost utter from material things, of the purely philosophical writer, whose balanced sentences move with a bloodless elegance which there is nothing subjective or tangential to impair. There might be a brusquer and more Anglo-Saxon way of expressing such material with no loss of the basic sense, but it is profitless to speculate how Heathcliff might have put it; Gabriel

Oak, less impassioned, hit on a native philosophical style as neat as Plato's when he summed up the happy marriage as 'at home by the fire, whenever you look up, there I shall be—and whenever I look up, there will be you', but profound and highly theoretical arguments are usually best expressed by long intellectual words from the Romance vocabulary.

So far, speaking as an admiring unphilosopher, I raise no objection to the existence of this arcane vocabulary for its own special deep purpose. But when there is no profundity to be expressed, and when the matter is the daily traffic of humans and their goods and concerns, the high style sits very uncomfortably. So an educationalist writes 'At the moment we want to couch our inquiry in very general terms. It is the case, for example, that consideration of a number of educational issues is already the province of departments in social science ... In Science and Mathematics, the educational implications of curricular and knowledge change are already very widely canvassed'; here some teaching schemes are being aired, a homely and man-to-man matter which would be more persuasively put in short, concrete terms. Unless we are offering the bland ruminations of a Bacon, or the burning eloquence of some great reformer, or the chilling intimacies of a psychologist recording what nobody else bothers to notice, or some other subject where things and people give place to concepts, then the heavily abstract style is wasteful, evasive, and inappropriate.

Its chief outward mark is nouniness. Mim and prissy fears for propriety prevent those perched on the branches of the Civil Service hierarchy from saying 'Aim high but realistically'; instead, 'Our target must be a concrete ceiling', with the dashed relish of a mixed metaphor. Sir Ernest Gowers, who writes so very well on abstractions in his *Plain Words* books, preferred *buy* to *purchase*, but his publishers tell us that the books are 'to be purchased from . . .'; mercifully, they do not then mention 'the usual trade channels'. How lucky the British Civil Service were to have such a colleague! He would never have been afraid of saying 'in a shop', where the noun, unlike 'trade channels', gives an immediate picture of what it represents. I was reading the other day that 'the inscription cannot be deciphered because of the worn nature of the stone'; but it isn't the 'nature' that is at fault—the decipherment is spoilt 'because the stone is worn'.

The spurious charm of long nouns is that they *are* long and impressive; they are a proof in themselves that we have accomplished the feat of knowing them, and statements made with them can never look like ordinary statements again. *The Army School of Equitation* has a dignity and skill that *riding-school* could not convey; but it was always a relief in more stately days to leave behind the English meat purveyors and cross the Scots Border to encounter the fleshers. He who devised the advertising slogan *Realistic Budget Fashions for Dignified Maturity* was either calculating or compassionate, but it does a worse job than does the frank and informative *Cheap Clothes for Fat Old Women* (as one good commentator translates it). In our day, when the dialogues and wars of religions, ideologies, classes and systems are being waged as much on paper as in the forum and the field, when universities have departments with names such as Econometrics and the Sociology of Education, and when many exact sciences have genuinely no other vocabulary than Latin and Greek compounds to express their findings, it is unavoidable that prose customarily drips with long nouns. But, outside the -isms, let us all try to give the verb and the red-blooded noun their place again. What would Alice Meynell do with the report 'The subject receives the reiterated impression that in the transitional stage between maximum consciousness and dormition she has an irresistible impulse to propel herself in a forward direction, resulting in an encounter with the amorous embraces of her former cohabitee'? She would vary it to

> With the first dream that comes with the first sleep,
> I run, I run, I am gathered to thy heart.

William Blake, giving us the clue in the title of his poem *The Human Abstract*, shows us there the emptiness of abstract virtues without human object: that pity need not exist if only we saw to it, by our efforts, that nobody was pitiable; we get out of realities and responsibilities by using abstract words. I have noticed further that sectarians whose principles rest on love for mankind rather than first on love for God can be very ardent in general but will sometimes be chilly, offhand, and vague, in their individual relationships.

The mind that hedges real objects and actions around with abstract nouns will also cover its retreat with passive verbs. It could be sensibly argued that when some known person performs some known action, then the best verb to express this is an active one: to say that 'this book was read by Chaucer' is inferior to 'Chaucer read this book', because the subject, the hero, the protagonist, of the sentence is he who performs the action. It is possible to feel immediate discontent with a sentence beginning 'It is estimated that . . .'; yet my last two sentences have begun (unnoticed, I should think) with these unnecessary *It*s, the first a peculiarly dull one where the popular *We could argue* . . . would be a more honest statement of the process, and the second a temporising way of saying *Perhaps*. Three adjacent sentences in a school's recent request for a reference go as follows: 'The successful candidate would be expected to maintain this tradition. Opportunities will be provided to teach English to "O" level: some "A" level work may be offered'; why all this caginess?—don't the people who run this school exist at all, or is it all done by silent machinery? The old, old schoolboy howler that 'active denotes action, as in *He kissed her*; passive denotes passion, as in *She kissed him*' is even further from the mark than its perpetrator knew, because these dehumanised sentences are passionless indeed. The same screed had a covering letter ending 'an early reply will be much appreciated'; I get a vague impression that, whereas they are making no promises of their own gratitude, a recording angel is impersonally putting something to my credit. Middle English shows less reticence and fewer passives; their common idiom was to use *mĕ* (a broken-down form of *man*, and equivalent to French *on*), as in *mĕ seith* ('one says', so 'it is said') or *mĕ thē bit* ('one offers thee', so 'thou art offered'), but I am not suggesting that the frequent use of *one* would now effect any improvement. When our interest is centred on the animate or inanimate object of an action, by all means let the verb fall into the passive; but many passives of the 'It is felt that' and 'It is meant to' type are totally unfelt and unmeant.

Another result of reluctance or evasiveness is to use negatives excessively. Only the uneducated say 'It doesn't hardly make sense', a virtual double negative, but there are some highly literate people who, with mathematical precision, string together negatives in a way that the reader or hearer finds hard to pair off and cancel out. I remember an academic in high authority who used to corner us and ask us questions such as 'Don't you think there's some doubt about the impracticability of abolishing the rule that forbids you to read English if you haven't "O" level Latin unless you're of mature age, but not rescinding the rule of not reading English without it at "A" level. . . ?' If you answered *Yes* to this, or *No* (having determined whether it was a *nonne* or a *num* question), he would shoot up his eyebrows and make it clear that he was astonished that you hadn't said *No*, or *Yes*. But sentences with two parallel negatives are always causing trouble, too, though the formula is simple: when two parallel parts of speech are preceded by negatives, the only correct phrasing is *not . . . or* or *neither . . . nor*; *Nor* can also begin a new statement after a negative statement. But the sequence *not . . . nor* is still wrong, despite its present vogue. Another oddity occurred in a *South Wales Echo* recipe in 1966, for making jelly lollies; I remember something about lolly moulds and freezing, and then came the doubtful recommendation 'These lollies do not melt and run down the arm when being eaten'.

Do we mean all our negatives, anyway? I am certain that we often say what we mean not: 'I don't think you're nice' irrelevantly negatives the thought, and would be franker as 'I think you're not nice'. So with *seem*: 'Nobody seems to have died of plague on the island for a hundred years' calls up irrelevant notions of only seeming to die, but even if we extricate it a little and make it 'It seems that nobody has died', the *seems* remains as an irritant, as if there were a false seeming; and the vagueness of it all is pointed by the fact that *seems that, seems as if,* and *seems as though,* are treated as equivalents. 'I can't seem to be able to concentrate' has the vicious features of tautology (*can . . . be able*), of the application of *not* to the wrong verb, and of this seeming for actuality.

Fowler and Gowers, who are so very practical and amusing when they treat such failures of logic, show us clearly how a writer loses his way in mid-construction; their ample illustrations can be matched wherever we have the opportunity to read or listen. How often in my hearing has the prudent mother told her child 'Sit down before you fall'!—she has no notion of the subjunctive, and we could argue that, since the end-product of her admonition is the child's not falling, 'Sit down before you don't fall' would serve better. A television tennis commentator spoke very darkly when he exhorted us as follows: 'We must wait and see whether Miss Wade makes too many mistakes to let her opponent profit by them'—an idiotic picture of more mistakes than the opponent can cope with, but restored to normal meaning by changing *to let* into *and lets.* I have seen quoted, but do not remember reading, a *Times* leader of 1951, 'The result of the General Election is not so surprising as might have been expected'; this breakdown of sense sounds too bad to be genuinely from *The Times,* and nothing will remedy it save the confidence that nothing which you expect is a surprise. Let me round off these wandering sentences with an eminent Reading advertisement; it is not strictly to our purpose, but it would make a lovely pendant to a chapter on almost anything: 'Ears Pierced While You Wait'.

12

STANDARD ACCEPTED JARGON

Sometimes all little birds that are,
How they seemed to fill the sea and air
With their sweet jargoning!

We are like Coleridge's Mariner in being exposed to
dozens of species all twittering or booming away in their
own jargons, specialised forms of language which are their
own concern, which they would not be so foolish as to use
if this was inconvenient, which have been trained and
trimmed by the centuries for express purposes, and which
we have no real right to greet with irritation, envy, mirth,
or contempt. I must say that, being happy with our
punctuation, I do not enjoy the lack of it in legal docu-
ments, but it would be foolhardy on my part to argue
against the wisdom of years; there is, indeed, real beauty
and balance in even the coldest reference to human beings
as the Law sees them:

> . . . provided nevertheless that if any such child or
> children has died or shall die in my lifetime leaving
> issue living at my death who attain the age of twenty-
> one years such issue shall stand in the place of such

deceased child and take per stirpes and equally between them if more than one the share of the proceeds
of sale which such deceased child would have taken if
he or she had survived and attained a vested interest
but so that no issue shall take whose parent is alive
and so capable of taking . . .

You will have gathered that I admire an unequivocal
and foolproof English, and the best legal language, composed in its guarded yet incantatory style, is with practice
neither difficult nor ugly to read; further, our punctuation,
vital in disordered prose with its various emphases and its
artfully placed phrasing, is hardly necessary in the well
marshalled ranks of legal terminology. It is easy to poke
fun at this language, by quoting its responsible and
exacting treatment of even the pettiest subject, or by roll-
ing off the cracked and yellow parchment terms of
spurious charters, blodwite and fledwite, tallage and
theam, infangthief and outfangthief and thirlmulture; but
this extreme jargon (we must use the term neutrally) is not
out to charm, or be popular, or talk in shorthand, and its
care and consistency are admirable.

To take another jargon which is even more freakish, and
positively recondite, we may do what seems a silly thing
and consider the language of heraldry. What, at first
examination, can this mannered and antiquated voice say
to us of any relevance at all? What on earth can 'Per pale
tenny and pean a fesse counterchanged' mean? Well, first,
heraldry has the most economical of all our jargons: without its pithy and epigrammatic force, we should have to
paraphrase this as 'a shield divided down the middle,
orange on the left-hand side and black with scattered gold

ermine tails and ermine spots on the right-hand side, with a horizontal bar running across which is black, etc, on the left and orange on the right'. But, secondly, it is the most consistent of all our jargons, too, a matter of great merit in view of the general state of the language; a 'blazon' or description of a shield can mean only one thing, and there is no other way to describe the shield. A computer scientist, Mr Fraser Duncan, assures me that heraldry has an algorithmic language as rigorous as any programming language, and that difficulties encountered by computer scientists in the 1960s, especially in relation to recursivity, had been solved for heraldry by heralds in the quite primitive days of their art.

It would actually be effrontery on my part to call medical and scientific English a jargon, once it is out of the quagmire of formulas and sesquipedalian words; this language is not trying to look pretty, but has a duty to be exact, clear, and in a highly conventional style. By this last epithet, I mean that researchers in one scientific field all over the world will recognise a pattern in which the material is presented; in reading medical dissertations for friends, I have noticed and approved the monotony of the presentation, the impassive neatness, the inexorable march of parallels in the various sad case-histories. It would be unthinkable for experimental scientists to be exposed to articles on the same subject by a scientific Macaulay on the one hand and a scientific e. e. cummings on the other; but where the subject is remoter from the laboratory, and concerned with scientific history or ethics, the prose can be of a high literary standard. The only editor who ever questioned a point in my English was in charge of a chemical journal; I am glad to say that we were both right. And it is humbling for Arts men, in their invincible and escapist ignorance of science, to find scientists such as the late Sir Harold Hartley, FRS, writing prose with as much panache, good taste, and industry as they. Yet I doubt whether simpler scientific research—the kind meanly called by high-powered scholars 'stamp-collecting' —need be recorded in a style so nerveless and repellent; the mere tabulations can be forgiven for having no aesthetic quality save symmetry, but the prose passages of description or argument often sound very funny to the outsider and cannot be very stimulating to the informed reader. Perhaps the research process of taking facts from a number of inaccessible places and stacking them together in another inaccessible place (this quip has many versions) deadens the prose, until it ceases to be prose and becomes a staccato catalogue of big accurate words hinged on little colourless ones.

I have only once in this book, I believe, given way to the word *journalese*. It is an ungracious word to use: week in, week out, or day in, day out, the journalist does his best to entertain, inform, convince, lull, a mixed lot of readers, on a variety of subjects and with the need for utmost haste. Whether editors still bite cigars and scowl up from under green eyeshades with 'I don't want it good; I want it Thursday' I do not know; but the continued pressure of this demanding and various task, all for a commodity which over many years sold for a penny or two, is bound to dull the freshness of the prose. It is easy enough for the leisured writer on specialist subjects to call the result journalese, but in this dismissal of a valiant all-round effort he is like the hateful little boy at the zoo who was shown the elephant, was told of its tonnage, its daily consumption of hay and water, the value of its tusks, its longevity and its prodigious memory, and then said ' 'Aven't 'e got lil eyes?' And journalists vary so: there are those magistral members of the profession who have qualified for acceptance by writing books of their own, by becoming real authors, and there are others who are tied to a useful and gentle routine in the provinces; *Punch* thought it funny to quote in 1939 the headline of a Workington newspaper: 'Outbreak of War Creates Profound Impression in Workington', but it must be seen that this is precisely what the news *did* do to the people, entitled to their feelings and fears, in a provincial town. Your Mercury cannot always wear golden-winged sandals or partake of the epic theme. The humblest newspapers will go on doing a decent job in a plain English, and some village-Harmsworth may well be a stylist as well as a shrewd observer of the local flower show and a vigilant guardian of the parish footpaths. So if funny things happen in your provincial paper, and in a London Stock Market slump 'the general gloom was sparked by a . . . loss on Wall Street overnight', be tolerant with the unpondered phrasing and enjoy it.

The task of the journalist is exacting, is performed in the glare of publicity, and is always suspected of partiality, lying, suppression, or exaggeration. And, of course, those who compile the 'party-orientated' newspapers have to cultivate that two-tier style by which a military retreat becomes a withdrawal to prepared positions; the trouble with a phrase such as 'neofascist lickspittle racist' is that it blares in on us as Epithet of Protest Mark IV and has no effect at all save to be tedious, and the trouble with 'Miss Fauncewaters Superb in Defeat on Centre Court' is that its graciousness cannot compensate for her, and the nation's, loss. Specialist journals, which weekly cope with the task of titillating specialist readers, face their monotonous idiom valiantly; fishermen are offered delicate modulations of *hooked/landed/bagged* and of expressions for weight and weather, and all this is neither comic nor contemptible. Many provincial newspapers are bound to be substantially jottings, with the main items conveyed in an ordinary narrative style; not so the rhetoric of that Sunday (of all days) paper which whets the reader's appetite with roundabout noun clauses: 'What happened when a popular raven-haired 22-year-old nursing sister missed her last bus was revealed at Guildford Crown Court today when . . .' Perhaps the worst single service that provincial papers do to our language is to allow and, I suppose, encourage the printing of memorial doggerel in their *In Memoriam* announcements; it is shameful that these verses, the insertion of people sincerely grieving (though hardly in the terms of the jingle), should be greeted by the discriminating reader as a hoot. But day after day the humble dead are recalled with sets of lines, sometimes a dozen from various sisters and cousins and aunts, in which we know that we shall find

> So tender, so true, so loving, so kind,
> What a beautiful memory left behind.

If the flippant reader is lucky, there may be an example of

> The angels said Come,
> The pearly gates opened,
> And in walked Mum.

III

And it is almost certain that someone will have 'gone to God's own/great/sweet garden. And left the door ajar'. This lot at least rhyme, whatever we may think of such goings-on in heaven; but all, mismetred and regular alike, make us regret this manifestation of the common style of poetry. Will no one tell them what they sing?

Let us leave journalists to their beleaguered, serviceable styles, in the final hope that they will try to exert a good influence rather than a catchpenny stimulus, that they will use less clichés, and that, if they *must* deceive by adjusting their words, they will do so either with more enjoyable subtlety or with more disarming transparency. But they lead me on to the English of advertising, a study which I know has been called the small change of linguistics; here is a jargon that lies all around us. It is a shuddering thought that, for many adults, who have forgotten even their *escape* from school, the telly offers the only heard rhetoric, and advertisements the only read rhetoric, of their lives—for the rest, they can skim the names and ages and weapons and sentences and mobs and teams and taxes and scores and strikes in the papers, because bingo and pools are nearly all numbers. Napoleon said that the English were a nation of shop-keepers, and although 'a nation of shop-lifters' is now more apt, it is certain that the language has been greatly and interestingly exploited by the mercantile class in the cause of persuasion to buy. This idiom has had its full-scale commentators (such as Vance Packard in *The Hidden Persuaders* and G. N. Leech in *English in Advertising*), and I believe that its more interesting aspect is the metaphysics of it rather than its specific linguistic experiments. Elegant and high-souled Arts graduates go in for marketing or advertising, and find themselves learning how to mishandle the language for material gain. I am reminded that a decent and straightforward young Arts man of my acquaintance had got himself into the false position of being trained in salesmanship by a soap firm. The instructor was pretending to be a small-front-room female general storekeeper, and my friend had to say 'With every canister comes this quality dishcloth'. He objected that he couldn't, that a dishcloth wasn't of 'quality'; he was told that he was 'too dogmatic', and he is now that great norm, a schoolmaster.

In the harsh, competitive world of advertising the whole truth is as a matter of course neither offered nor expected, though it often occurs by coincidence. Even obviously true statements are sometimes deceitful, as taking no account of many imponderables; understatements are meant to convince of deep sincerity. Most of us feel more at ease in the presence of frantic boast and foolish word. The very simplest statements do not wrench or strain the sinews of the language; they can be downright pleased with themselves ('W. H. Smith & Son Sell Most Books'), or whisperingly modest ('this unobtrusive little table-wine' and her sisters). They can certainly be very snobbish; some kind of shirt is 'for the man who won't settle for second-best'; a home swimming-pool is 'Status symbol, luxury living, call it what you like'; and there is the unimaginable bathos in the last word of 'From the craftsmen who have created so many individually blended cigarettes'; or we are cut down to size by an ambassadorial-looking gentleman saying to a footman 'If you have any, I should like a White Horse'. If I had to categorise the other methods, short of literal truth, which neither are figurative nor play games with the strange resources of our tongue, I should do so by developing a classification somewhat as follows:

(1) *Hyperbole*. Having leant over backwards to say 'Dab washes whiter than white', the advertisers have nothing left to say when their new secret formula leaves the drawingboard, and resort to 'Now NEW Dab washes whiter than ever before'; the word *biological* is applied freely—we await the first flake to have a hydrogen warhead. There is also the vicious hyperbole of *great* as applied to alcohol and nicotine products—'the great lager', 'the great little cigarette':

> Men are we, and must grieve when even the shade
> Of that which once was great, has passed away.

(2) *Innuendo*. 'Doesn't contain digitalis'—well, nor do other brands; they couldn't and wouldn't, but now the seed of doubt is sown, and the ignorant mind is left with the feeling that they *do*, though of course with no understanding of what the effect would be if they *did*. The opposite of this is mere innuendo, too, because when a genuine scientific name is dropped, as if carelessly ('Contains gardol'), it is the merest hint but it trades beautifully on impressionable mindlessness; after all, I can remember the first public impact of chlorophyll, which adjusted every antisocial state from halitosis to perspiration. Or a little folksy word is used to deceive; in the late 1940s a seed firm was advertising 'Send for specimens of our gorgeous moonflower'; it turned out to be convolvulus, no boon in any garden. The same contempt for the consumer's good sense is shown in the now frequent notice 'Practical Chimneysweep'. I am assigning 'Fluologist' to

an altogether superior class of advertising, because it makes a pretty and witty show out of a grubby job; but a theoretical chimneysweep is of no interest to anyone, and the notice is a nasty reminder of that absurd (albeit Coleridgean) phrase 'practical criticism'. Someone I know has a 'fully automated' windowcleaner calling.

(3) *Decency*. When a product is worthy, it is agreeable and convincing to read the decent, clean-limbed, sturdy, elemental wording that promotes it. It is satisfying to see wool praised under the heading 'Ever heard of a cold sheep?', and the technique is or was used also for herb remedies and things like Mother Siegel's Syrup and Joe Wells's Athletic Rub. Its fatuousness comes out in challenges like that of some tobacco, 'Are you ready for it yet?', or of some liquor, 'The beer the *men* drink' (picture of husky, tanned, hirsute, sweating polo-player, skindiver, yachtsman, etc), or of some after-shave cosmetic, 'The smell that instantly says MAN'. I reserve my especial contumely for the more recent beer slogan, 'Thass wot yer right arm's *for*'; oh, the dignity of labour!

(4) *Lying*. Mere transparent misrepresentation is naturally rare; even the notorious toothpaste of which one couldn't buy a small tube, the only sizes being large, extra large, and jumbo, could claim that other brands went in for smaller sizes, so *large* meant *comparatively* large. The principal use of downright mendacity is in estate agents' descriptions of houses, where the courtly statements can often be counterpointed by the sceptical mind with a sort of translation or, shall we say, another way of looking at things: 'The opportunity exists (*we've been trying to sell the place to any buyer for a year*) to acquire (*well, don't make it*

sound as if it came free) a house of character (*dilapidated*), capable of conversion (*totally unwieldly*), in a secluded position (*no made-up road to it, and hemmed in by a quarry on the other side*), four miles from main-line station (*due for closure*), with wide views (*on top of a hill facing the prevailing north-easterlies*), Old English garden (*Polygonum cuspidatum and four lupins*), paddock (*scruffy little grassless plot*), available utilities (*ugh, those pylons!—and why doesn't he mention the drains?*), two oak-panelled reception rooms (*wood-worm?—dry-rot?*), utility room (*no windows*), playroom (*no door*), six bedrooms (*four with quaint sloping roofs, and sky-lights*) . . .', and so on. But the prose is often admirable

(5) *Fiction.* The narrative type of advertisement was usually conveyed (it is rarer now) in dialogue and with pictures singly or in strips: little dramas, homely or sophisticated, in a fairly authentic colloquial idiom. Horlick's, especially, used to mount highly interesting half-page near-tragedies, which observed the unities of time, place, and action, and which starred impatient mothers, unhelpful librarians, testy policemen, soured midwives, negligent bridge-builders, and other anomalous heroes and heroines who came out tops in the end by con-quering night starvation and ensuring deep, sound sleep. In the older days, all you were given was one picture; but the sharp cry of 'I love to dance, but oh! my feet' for many years boosted the sale of some corn solvent. Nor were our feelings spared: a really haunting sequence in an American magazine showed how Elmer had 'hickies' (I understand that these are American things like pimples) and was cured, and soon married, by the application (or was it the imbibing?) of a brand of yeast. How much more

refined was the British recommendation, repeated week after week with a new girl's Christian name and new faces, for a face-cream, and always to the formula '*Darling, you look tired*, he said. He meant to be kind, but Deirdre knew that a tired look is an old look'; the name was never the plebby, filmstar kind.

(6) *Fantasy and myth* have long been exploited, especially by Guinness's. Although a tireless teetotaller, I must admit that their scenes from, say, *Alice in Wonderland*, in lavish colour and with an intense closeness of parody, seemed civilised enough for *Country Life* and even for their frequent position facing the pretty-lady frontispiece; the name, by many tags and by the erection of an elaborate mystique, has certainly been fixed in the reader's mind. But whether Schweppes could succeed by their variation of this technique, I strongly doubt; it is one thing to appreciate Stephen Potter's myth of Schweppeshire and Schwepherd's Pie and the poet Percy Bysshe Schwelley, and quite another to carry away a clear impression of what it's 'all in aid of'. Still, it was very enjoyable.

(7) *Gnomes* (not the kind that fish in people's gardens), wise saws, and apothegms. A few old advertising tags had the good fortune to become, as it were, proverbial; and, though they perished at the impact of high-pressure slogans in recent years, 'Good morning, have you used Pears' Soap?' and 'He won't be happy till he gets it' must have been worth a million to Pears. 'The Man from the Prudential' is still with us, after a very long time. There is nothing intrinsically good, from a linguistic or literary standpoint, about these tags, but they must have been timely, their goods had few rivals at the time, and they

stuck, becoming phrases independent of advertising, as does their modern counterpart 'I'm only here for the . . .' (would not 'I'm here only for the . . .' be better?).

(8) *Politeness.* So much of our selling technique is now rough and vulgar (like the drab slang of huge block letters saying that some silly trifle is the 'zippiest, zingiest, swingingest' available) that it is well to remember how polite it can be, too. They want to sell chewing-gum to nice people; but the champing jaws of the vulgar, and the casual occurrence of the end-product on pavements and cinema seats, have given it a bad image. So there's a picture: a group of lithe, lean, inbred, aristocratic males in a Royal Box or a cricket pavilion or a vast ballroom with their female counterparts, and the warning 'Naturally, no one would think of using chewing-gum in these circumstances; but . . .' And then it suggests stocking up for those private junctures when one may chew unblamed. But the politeness is often mere euphemism, as with the 'Realistic Budget Fashions for Dignified Maturity'; it was amusing to see how the whispered and unmentionable 'BO' gently established itself in our vocabulary.

I have tried to depict the spirit of advertising in its various manifestations, almost ignoring the wretched slang by which trade does such harm to the language; even when the wording is not contemptibly vulgar, it can reduce vogue words to meaninglessness by repetition: the Fantastic Value, Fabulous Bargains, Unique Offer, Unrepeatable Prices, Yours for only 35p and two labels. But trade also subjects words and phrases to specific linguistic experiments, often to the enrichment of our tongue; so, with contrived euphony, we get pretty made-up sounds like Dreft, Chilpruf, Kiddicar, Tottipot. And it is possible that firms with multiple partners have exploited the poetry of their names; small wonder that Hillier, Parker, May and Rowden have been made the first line of a lovely narrative lyric about climbing the highest mountain in Wales. There is *authority* in the consortium of Knight, Frank and Rutley, and an awful feeling of crossing the Rubicon in accepting a post through Gabbitas and Thring. Three partnered sweetmeat-manufacturers liked their names so much that they ran their first letters into *Clarnico*, rather as newlyweds call their bungalows Ronkath and Lilbert; and the musing mind, playing with the Abbey National Building Society, erects the whimsical echoic characters Happy National, Nappy National, Abbey Natural, Cabby National, and so on. There can be contrived cacophony, too, equally effective in its context: Slugdeath has a charnel sound, and Smith's Crisps crackle appetisingly. Rhymes and jingles are pressed into service, and prove memorable; long ago we were admonished that 'An apple a day/Keeps the doctor away', and now British Rail try to win back passengers with The Brain Train, The 'I'll See You Again' Train, and Trains For Planes. My strongest memory of the first Highland Games I ever saw, at Nairn, is not of cabers and pipes but of a melancholy-looking little man trudging round and round the field, almost airborne by a huge tray of pink candy-floss and wailing 'Candy for Sandy'. With rhyme is linked the more native idiom of alliteration: Mac Fish Fresh Fish is brisk and quite unforgettable, and with it goes a happy, smiling fish (you know, they *like* being caught by MacFisheries), and I further commend the fine heraldic device of *azure a saltire between four herrings naiant within a bordure argent.* So with Weaver to Wearer, Brooke Bond, Basildon Bond, My Goodness my Guinness, Glaxo Builds Bonny Babies, Pink Pills for Pale People, Fisons Pharmaceuticals, Sunny Southsea, Pretty Prestatyn, Beer is Best, Keating's Kills, Players Please, Tiger in my Tank: anyone who does not momentarily enjoy this manipulation of the language is pedantic or mirthless.

Double entendre is a very old device in advertising. One of the eminent posters of the 1930s was for Reckitt's blue—a yacht against a hyacinthine blue sky and sea, with white foam in its wake and the wholesome legend 'Out of the blue comes the whitest wash'. There, the coincidence was in the meanings of two nouns; in 'Next to yourself you'll like Vedonis', the joke hinges on the literal and figurative uses of the prepositional phrase *next to*; in the travel poster 'Greece/Remains to be Seen' the regrettable equivalence of plural noun and singular verb is put to work. 'Go to Work on an Egg' we have been told, and alcohol firms in their frantic rivalry come out with things like 'Rhymney Beer—the Best Round Here' (*round* noun or *round* = 'around'). The angels sometimes have their own back: a nice double use of the preposition *for* produces 'One for the road may mean two for the hospital', and a filthy ashtray filled with beery and lipsticky fag-ends carries the warning 'The best tip—give it up!' The liberties taken with our grammar can be very enjoyable: 'Beanz Meanz Heinz' is a splendid device, and the Janus-headed pedestrian muttering with admiration 'That's Shell, that was' remained an old favourite despite his ignorance of the sequence of tenses. Although I never liked the repeated jests like the Uneeda Hairclip, I think that the Drinka Pinta has plenty of quality; it frankly admits the falling together into ə of so many of our vowels, and it has nobly raised the honest pinta as a rival to the insidious pint. But made-up hybrids used without an alert sense of humour are not always as effective as they are meant to be: I have seen outside Cardiff a café called Daiswill (apparently a she-and-he name like Lilbert), where the last five letters prompt second thoughts, and in the suburbs of nearby Newport there was a woolshop with the insensitive word NITCRAFT on its facia-board. The coining of portmanteau words with more care gives us acceptable new forms like Chilpruf, Snowcem, Instamatic, and Forgettle; but *not*, please, a Tudorbethan Cottabunga such as was advertised in 1967 in East Suffolk and caused a newspaper editor to comment that we could soon be having a 'magnadull offiblock' and a 'deadlimod concrilump'. And placing is vital: a house in St Paul's Road, Clifton, Bristol, put to office use, formerly bore an alarming postcard-shaped notice board with two big panels inscribed

| M. ZATTMAN | People's Dispensary |
| Furrier | for Sick Animals |

This may seem a very long disquisition on the often sub-literary art of advertising; but the texts which it seeks to categorise are thrust upon us in the street, in the 'bus or tube, in the newspaper, and (if we use one) on the television screen. Advertising offers a linguistic study where we can live off the land, and our alertness in assessing what we have read may make us less credulous shoppers. But we are exposed even more to the 'media', a word which apparently can be treated as singular or plural. I have no television set, and my only belief about it is that the State should provide colour television sets to all incapacitated people who need a vicarious existence; I haven't even what I still call a wireless set. Yet the influence of the 'media' washes over me, because I am a citizen of the world and everyone else is influenced by it/them. Television is not yet compulsory; its older sister is, in the form of a kind of music on any hot summer beach (I shall not say that this is a foretaste of hell) or as produced from little black instruments by neighbours fettling their cars in the road. Since the viewer can still be eclectic, he can often improve his English by listening to good scripts in the standard dialect, well delivered and politically temperate; the speaker may sometimes feel it his duty to subdue his personal involvement, and so his voice may flatten and lack enthusiasm, but the better announcers and regular speakers, even those who appear to break rules of tempo and facial gesture, are models of how the language could still sound. Unhappily, drama can set no such standard; it has been decided that the public want to see and hear ignorant poverty in its own setting. The Magnificat promise to the humble, meek and hungry is too often translated into an exposure of them as trapped and monotonous, and incoherent on any subject save sex, where they can be remarkably vocal. Their more affluent working-class brethren (the term must be used, though they are shown at work no more than the characters in a Jane Austen novel) occur in dramas that move in and out of taverns, dubious garages, flashy clubs, and the stock genre flat with one Tretchikoff, three diminishing ducks, a cocktail-cabinet, and a bitsy japanned upright telephone. The English in which all this is conveyed must have done much harm; its mixture of RADA, uneasily assimilated

Cockney and Brum and Liverpuddlian, some Mummerzet when the adulterous pair in the stolen car reach country parts, and sheer foul-mouthed artificiality, is held up as the dynamic patter whereby the frustrated viewer can attain the cocktail-cabinet, the bird, the backgammon outfit, and the big car that can turn on a sixpence ('whatever *that* is', as Gulbenkian is supposed to have said).

Drama used to be classed as literature, and intellectuals as those who thought about something other than sex for part of the time. Middle-class drama, whether inflicted weekly or in isolation, shows the same skill in its mounting, the same ingenuity in its interlocking narratives, a greater authenticity in its idiom and accent, and far less gore, but still a strong line in lust; a friend of mine, whose wife was hebdomadally tied to a very pullulating and orchidaceous thing called *Compact*, about a women's magazine, used to call it *Compost*. It is coming to something, as Shaw would agree, when it is only upper-class drama that gives any lead in morals and standards, a task traditionally reserved for the bourgeoisie, with the working classes as a second line of defence; but it seems probable that in recent years plays and serials about the privileged have done rather little harm by their morals and considerable good by their English, when it is imitable.

For the speech of the 'media' is certainly imitated. It must sometimes lead to greater richness of vocabulary, to the correction of persistent faults of pronunciation, and to the reception of all programmes as if they were part of the Open University course; this is the happier view, but it cannot be common. The baser phrasing has a quick and easy appeal; a man arrested a couple of years ago for a shooting at a bank said 'Not me, man; I don't dig this', which was current idiom but sounds like imitation of some sincerely admired character of fiction. The formula is both callous and slovenly, and in the same way a male whom I heard on television saying 'Gladys, I fancy you something rotten' was not using an idiom usually selected; yet in its fatuous wrongness it seems to me a good phrase as an antidote to the swooning lasciviousness that sees even church towers as fertility symbols.

The 'media', and other forms of public report, have given us over the years many jerked-out phrases, some neat and strong, some flaccid—and all jargon and hackneyed. Who started 'I couldn't care less?'—it was the password of an uncaring generation, so the moralists said; it is certainly ill put, because it bears the additional meaning 'I couldn't possibly find it in my heart to be any more unfeeling'. 'Roll on' means nothing at all; 'they just don't wanna know' covers the likelihood that 'their point of view (to which I am blind) differs from mine'; 'not to worry' is pointlessly asyntactical. There is no harm, save for its vogue, in '*Now* he tells me!', a neat and wry little protest deriving from the humour of the American Jews. I am growing weary of 'Nudge, nudge!'; but I remember growing similarly weary, years ago, of females who said something catty or arch and then added 'Said she'. These snatches of speech, beginning as wit and ending as cliché, are sometimes ephemeral and sometimes lasting; most of them are good-humoured, even when their origins are ghastly, as with 'Ve haff vays to make you talk', but some are unpleasant, like the rebuff to someone trying to decide on a course of action, 'Yes, *do that*', with strong emphasis that points the indifference. No rancour should be detected in the pretended threat of 'You can go off people, you know!', and various terms such as '*orrible* and *beast* and 'You can't take him anywhere' have become almost terms of endearment. How we judge the merit of these sayings, and whether we even find ourselves using them, probably depends on the circumstances, blithe or boring, in which we first heard them, and the acquaintance who preceded us in knowing them. I disliked 'Long time no see' intensely until the lovely report that it was the greeting that the Pope gave to the Archbishop of Canterbury (this is very subtle); but I still think that 'Be my guest' and 'Feel free' are unwelcoming and sardonic, and that 'You have to be joking' sounds very sour. 'I like it', in appreciation of a jolly joke or some diverting true narrative, has displaced the 'I rather care for that' of the 1940s. I neither know nor greatly care where these sayings originated; I am mainly concerned that they should not take charge of our idiom of familiarity and pleasantry.

Even without 'the box' (a blunter cliché than 'the idiots' lantern') we have always coined our comic snippets on a wide range of subjects; facial appearance has been one of the chief sufferers, with 'a face like the back of a 'bus', 'a face like an open grave', and 'he looked like death warmed up'. These have long lost whatever charm they had, and I was refreshed and repelled to hear the other day, at Caldicot in South Wales, 'a face like a ripped dap' (it should be explained that *dap* is Anglo-Welsh for a plimsoll or running-pump). This, despite its high imagination, will never find its way into literature, and other regional grotesqueries will have to remain undiscovered and unadopted. In my childhood I used to hear an old woman from near Swansea characterise any indifferent housewife thus: 'She couldn't make a shirt for a shovel'; it was funny the first time, with its extra alliterative force, and it has the merit of the best similes in its unexpected reconciling of disparate objects, but it may have been handed down as a waspish joke over generations of mothers and daughters. Such rustic wit has retained at least a little alertness; and its tightness makes its imagery far more palpable than the ludicrous use of *through* ('on account of') makes the literal statement by the mother of a spotty child: 'His face is coming up through his stomach'. I wonder whether a bright and very robust corporal was quoting or creating when he told me in 1945 that his mate had thrown himself face downward in the mud during a shelling, and 'picked himself up like a piece of sticking-plaster'; this is brilliantly apt.

The superior version of this figurative language is the speech that adroitly weaves in quotations. Some commentators on speech condemn those who use phrases such as 'my custom always in the afternoon' even when *not* referring to the obvious taking of a nap, and it is easy to criticise those who call any large body of females a 'monstrous regiment', since this shows ignorance of semantics. Or we show how up-to-date we are, by reference to bang and whimper, or coffee-spoons, or (with that awe-inspiring range that characterises our reading) 'rather mere'; this firmly roots us in the twentieth century—we do not have to be 'dragged screaming' into it. And so on. The Fowler-Gowers attack on this sort of thing is made in a scatter of articles that harshly show the irrelevance, the tedium, the ostentation, the sheer incompetence in speaking directly, that attend the use of all clichés from scholarly references down to the figures of folk speech. Yet in the *Radio Times* of 27 June 1974 a person called Jill

Hyem, mentioning the need for 'articulate' people in a programme, laid it down that 'Working-class people tend not to be so articulate, they talk in clichés. We could get one in, say, if he'd been to a red-brick university'.

This statement grows sillier phrase by phrase (and divides two sentences by a comma). The generalisation 'working-class', even when we try to define it more closely as 'those whose jobs are dull or dirty or dangerous or all three', still covers and omits too many people, and too many attitudes to work and leisure, for us to accept it; the speaker admits that they only 'tend' to have difficulty in expressing themselves. As for their use of clichés, the supposed class next above them can come out with whole tissues of clichés, which work their way down from their minutes, directives, balance sheets, fashionable reading, party small-talk, and natural caution; they *can* be so cliché-ridden that even Christian love is called a 'caring situation', a phrase where the principle of charity is diluted and paled. We need not for the moment follow this lady into her arrogant assumption that a 'worker' might make it to a red-brick institution, and that this would improve his speech; I am concerned with two facts—that all 'classes' use their own insipid types of cliché, obtained in increasing numbers from the 'media', and that her statement is divisive and class-haunted. Earlier in this book, I urged that we should write good letters as if we were engaged in sincere conversation, and should converse as if we were writing good letters; now let all men and women, of whatever 'class', speak up clearly and honestly, using of themselves the exact phrases that they mean, and not from the 'media' the English that they are too lazy or too impressed to recognise as the pinchbeck stuff it is. For *desiderate*, for *most* when we mean 'very', and for *individual* when we mean 'man' or 'woman', there is no excuse at all.

I must take up the glum idea that attendance at a university would file a worker's speech into a shape satisfactory to the 'media'. It should certainly extend vocabulary, reassure hesitation, sharpen perception, remove grossness, and live up to various other Johnsonian phrases, and in most cases this happens; but whereas years ago the English that we dreaded from students' essays was phrasing like 'a sheer cascade of lyrical ravishment', we now occasionally encounter him or her who must, on doctrinaire grounds, show no patience with élitist wording or delivery. If these young people use a *thank you* formula at all, it is 'Chiz', and they give assent by 'Yeah'; on the other hand, the polysyllabic cant of their chosen theorists comes easily to them, especially in relating the machinery and resolutions of their 'quorate' and other meetings. I am not just confounding their politics, but pointing out that their English is an ineffective mixture of the lightweight and the leaden. The average 'worker' speaks more pleasantly and to better purpose; I want Britain to be run by neither stockbrokers nor shopstewards, and their English (as published) would come under my censure, too. The language of business, big and small, was always at the other end of the line from induced uncouthness; it used to be unctuous and formulaic, and its recommended opening gambits, such as 'Your favour of the 21st inst. to hand, thanks for same, which is receiving our best attention', were notorious, but the pressures of modern industry and marketing have squashed all the frills. The duplicity can remain, and 'which is receiving our best attention' can still mean 'we have lost your order somewhere in our files';

expedite conveys anything or nothing. But the false courtesy is no loss, and the influence of war-time adjutant's English—'personnel will not, repeat NOT'—may have been salutary in concerns that were governed as a well ordered unit.

I am assuming that the political language of the main parties, when it is tainted with tergiversation, cheap invective, and the big words of theory, doesn't warrant our notice; the little parties show the same forked tongues, but with less publicity. But why must trade union officials speak so ill? If they spoke merely with regional accents, with unpolished phrases, with unschooled simplicity, with bitter earnestness, with practical commonsense, with a command of their complicated history, with precision in conducting delicate negotiations, with the fluency and earnestness of conviction, and with a rejection of allusive or figurative language, they would deserve all the more respect and a hearing. Theirs, however, is often the worst officialese, by a two-fold technique: first, their spokesmen take on polysyllables as Laocoön and his boys took on the serpents, reluctantly and to their own throttling. Secondly, the intervals between their rumbling abstract nouns are filled with those long-winded equivalents of *er* which some public speakers, and far too many conversationalists, use to preclude interruption and to occupy those moments of silence when there might be a time for doubt: 'Speaking for myself personally, and in the ultimate analysis, in this day and age and at this particular moment in time, by and large, as yet . . .' Of course, we all use these fill-in phrases; without meaning or necessity, we dull our speech, and arouse suspicion, with assertions of veracity: *in fact, the fact is, as a matter of fact, the fact of the matter is*. All these are

I 129

no more than a kind of tick, a sign for the sentence to go on and get on with it, but we may add *I mean to say, Let's face it, to be frank with you, to be quite candid with you, to be quite frank and honest with you, to tell you the truth, to put you in the picture, to give you a breakdown of the situation, to fill you in with the details* . . . A cure for this habit might be to repeat to ourselves strings of these vaporous phrases until they make us giggle. Nobody is 'himself' in using them, and they sound like sustained humbug; let public speakers who wish to convince us of their own honesty avoid them, ignore the long Latinisms, and be themselves.

Be as little children? To what source do the innocent and uninhibited turn for replenishment of their word-hoard, to what inspiration do they look in their dawning literary and communicative activities? Mainly to the telly and the tranny, but also to the comic; the comic has the more venerable history, but must have grown repetitious over the years, since there is a limit even to the variations of canonised naughtiness and amusing violence. The comic is not educational save when it is the only text which the child is willing to read; it is used as a kind of dummy or tranquilliser on long journeys, and its gaudy colours and explicit pictures make the reading an optional extra. But its older brothers and sisters, so often well intended, have perished; what child from ten to fourteen would now read every word and study every picture of the sober and civilised *My Magazine*, brought out diligently every month by Arthur Mee?—he was also engaged on the less literary but highly responsible *Children's Newspaper* week by week; both were dedicated to a concept of the Empire and of the League of Nations which the years have effaced, and both were tinged at times with the rather twee style that ruins

his county topographies *The King's England*, but they always *had* a style (and a moral standard, which is not our
concern). There was also a style, and a maddeningly consistent one, in the weekly products of Frank Richards, the
creator of Greyfriars School and other seats of the same
foundation; the decent striplings, and the famous fatling,
who peopled these places were (I am glad and grateful to
say) on my parents' Index, though I heard my less protected schoolfellows as they jabbered about Bunter, the
fatuous owl of the Lower Remove. It is an arresting thought
that Frank Richards ('. . . unmarried . . . *Recreations*: chess;
the classics, especially Horace and Lucretius; music . . .',
Who's Who) is said to have been the most prolific writer of
English recorded, his words running into millions and
millions; likewise the dire Enid Blyton is supposed to have
been the most translated writer in the world apart from
Marx and Lenin—I don't know what this proves, and I
should think that Moses, David, Paul, and the rest of that
consortium, run her pretty close. Periodicals for children
have certainly changed, and many of them are deplorable;
but parents who care about their children's reading can
find plenty of bright, well written books on any subject
that charms, or informs, or even saves from the vociferous
tyranny of the record.

I have mentioned, and in part examined, a selection of
the current jargons, suggesting that most of them have a
right to exist and sometimes even a special power which
the outsider cannot fully share. I would exclude graffiti,
written or sprayed higher up the wall since the raising of
the school-leaving age, and Cockney rhyming slang,
whereby you call your friend an *oppo* because *chum* rhymes
with *Hop o' my Thumb*. But of all the private languages,

closed except to those who are willing to study and to attain understanding, the best and clearest should be the language of criticism, whether of literature or music or drama or the visual arts. Page 6 of the very first number of *Scrutiny* said that 'more people are able to write good criticism than good verse or short stories'; more people are willing to, as well—but I must not risk uttering fearful heresies like 'the critic must be himself a practitioner'. Whatever my views on this, I am still minding my own business if I require that 'the critic must be himself a stylist'.

The great provinces of criticism are peopled by writers of strangely different dispositions, attitudes, and standards. The musicologist has rarely much, and never wholly, enjoyed the concert which he has attended. Forgetting how he has spoilt his neighbours' enjoyment by crisply turning the pages of his score every few bars, he expresses a kind of sympathy and tolerance at the efforts of the orchestra, but the conductor took *this* movement too fast and *that* one without 'authority', the woodwinds didn't come out of the allegretto at all well, and one passage (as I recall) 'bristled with *rubato*'; or, if he is dealing with new recordings, he makes a few of them sound unsaleable and the highbrow ones obligatory. The art critic is far happier at his work, but his enthusiasm isn't always catching; what he has to say, especially of modern art, is wholly for the converted, and is too often offered in a take-it-or-leave-it spirit. He has an inescapable way of sounding 'pseudo'; even when we have worked out the mathematics of *cinquecento*, admitted that we are not the 'we' who 'are reminded of Dosso Dossi', and accepted that a hunk of phosphor-bronze with a hole in it and called *Composition*

1974 is 'superb', we remain uninformed and resentful—
we are still excluded from the mysteries within the shrine.
The dramatic critic has seen the old play done better, or
differently, or by actors from a destroyed mould, and there
is something about his knowing style that makes us envy
his leisure, his scope, his hobnobbing; or, with the new
play, we have to share his bewilderment or his marvellous
tolerance, especially when there is no plot, only 'be-
haviouristic incident'—but he is an expansive fellow, and
handsomely cosmopolitan. Now the literary critic is
altogether more friendly and helpful than these: with a
wide range of duties to accomplish—pure criticism, exe-
gesis, literary biography, or the genuinely clever work of
the *comparatiste*—he can write in as many acceptable styles,
and can mantle himself as reformer, or prophet, or wag in
motley. His task is vast, but his opportunities are lavish. If
he is by real inclination a social historian, his tastes may
'show', but valuably for his critical purpose; if he is equally
at home in a foreign language, his skill may shed a clearer
light on the English which he discusses; if he has religious
or ethical or political leanings, his critical prose may be
the more strenuously argued and, at points, the more
sensitive. He must not, of course, show off, citing peri-
pheral disciplines instead of adhering to the text, and
behaving like a peripatetic Joint School of a dozen subjects:

> All the supposititious mystery
> Of music, politics, and history,
> Philosophy divine and human,
> Schumann and Truman, Hume and Newman.

He must not show off in *any* way; the oracular will resemble the orotund. The world can wait for his next critical article; the call to the dustman is imperious and immediate. A body of criticism is not a Scripture for a godless generation; it is merely by a pen-pusher about pen-pushers. If it makes claims too large, it may lose its reasonable reputation for transmitting and clarifying great ideas and great compositions, the holy and humane tasks for which it is qualified. To call the undertaking of a literary MLitt thesis a 'job of work' is to give it the wrong colour; it is variously a refined pastime, a rung in one's career, a further lingering in Arcady, an extension of the bounds of culture and knowledge, and a training in teaching others, but it is not dull, dirty, or dangerous, and should never be the occasion of woe, as it so often is. Equally, the established critic or textual scholar must take himself seriously, but not make a fortress of himself; those who question his views are his partners in a great civilising endeavour, not his foes, for criticism and the literature which is its subject are not a battlefield or a work-camp—or, by the way, an industry. The world that can wait for his next critical article to mature is not bound to enjoy with *his* pleasure his public trouncing of someone who has differed from him on a point of interpretation. Those who are determined to treat literature, and its description, as an industry should at least let the labour relations in it be smooth; though, as far as I am concerned, treating universities as factories that are 'turning out' students or studies is in the same bad taste as calling church buildings and church resources 'plant'.

As I probably made clear just now, the reason that I stop short of demanding a practitioner-critic is that the matter could be called irrelevant in the present context;

but I am positive that any critic whose style of writing is poor should desist. This is not to ask for sustained coruscation or elegance; but if his prose is tortuous and jerky, or —worse—ambiguous and cacophonous, he disqualifies himself from a hearing on the achievements of other writers. If he uses to death a word that at its first occurrence was hale (*ambivalent* or *charisma*), or inserts false words like the nasty *viable* and *frequenting* a poem, he must try to recognise that he has these favourite words, and to avoid them. And let him be somewhat Laodicean: the engendering of great heat is out of place in literary criticism, but so is a frigid detachment; he must convey and share delight and understanding, and this cannot be done in the arid, camouflaged style of a stick-insect communicating with its mate.

It may cause surprise that my study of language has not mentioned the science of Linguistics or its expression. I submit that it is mainly a philosophical enquiry, and one with strong political and sociological overtones. It shows no love of our language, only a wish to dissect it; its terms are mathematical or barbarous, though its arguments are likely to be very clever. A current catalogue invites me to buy a book 'reorganizing the subject in terms of generative-transformational grammar, and aiming both to reduce concepts to their most basic components and to interrelate them', and another 'providing comprehensive coverage of sociolinguistics and applied linguistics, as well as communication, form and function, meaning, and grammatical theory'. I heard a Linguistics man call teaching 'a communicative event'; true, but chillingly put.

13

THE DELICATE SUBJECT OF STYLE

It should be easy, on the subject of prose style, to say very little and for that little to be the obvious; to hope that there is a general agreement on what is clear and euphonious; and to accept a common style as the best means of report and as the link between those expert studies which together form knowledge not arithmetically but by their dovetailing. The existence of this common style requires the sloughing of all 'stylishness' from style, and an excellent *lingua franca* results which can be shared by all writers and readers who do not need titivations and shocks to keep them going. This is the prose of, say, Sir Arthur Bryant, a prose weighty but free-moving, ready for narrative or for pondering, always capable of the purple patch but never condescending to the meretricious moment. (But, soft!—I have alliterated, on *p c p p c m m*; was that enjoyable or distasteful, glaring or unnoticed?). A plea for a common style of prose is not, of course, a plea for mediocrity; genius (a word that has not yet belonged to this long discourse on a threatened language) will put excellent material to its own purpose. If 'style' means anything at all, its shapers will ensure that no desultory evenness is spread like butter or piped like icing on to the language, but that the richness and adornments will ooze from the hearts of writers themselves.

How shall their intense individuality be served? Once we escape from the old idea that all great poetry must be metaphorical, we next may well question whether it is by the figures of relating and identifying that the prose-writer best shows his powers of vision, sensitiveness, and real novelty. It must be remembered that in speech and everyday prose the commonest metaphors are the dead ones, dull at best and mixed at worst. Some of the oldest unchanged words in the language are those for which there is no substitute and which do not easily lend themselves to a transferred use; but we won't leave words intact—the oldest French borrowings, extant already before 1066, should be inalienable, but have been pressed into metaphors even while keeping their literal meaning: 'he saved his *bacon*', 'Tory *ginger* group', '*tower* of strength', 'it'll *serve* my purpose', 'the nail is a bit *proud*', 'he's be*sotted* over her'. There might have been more stability if Hobbes had had his way as expressed in Chapter V of *Leviathan*, and metaphors had been avoided: we might have had one word, one meaning. But it isn't *our* doing, after all, that words shift their planes, and swell or shrivel; whole books have been written on the naughty escapades of one single word. One of the best is my old colleague Susie Tucker's *Enthusiasm*, a word that started by meaning that you had a 'god in' you, was eventually pejorative, and has now become a piece of commendation, as in 'commendable enthusiasm'. Such a study requires examination of all the linguistic company that the word has kept, plotting of all the dated uses, and of course record of any deliberate attempts to stabilise its reference. It is all this that makes the use of metaphor even trickier: with every word, not just the metaphorical, the exploitation of ambiguity depends on the historical accumulation of multiple meanings, and the meaning of a word can be something delightfully indeterminate.

Nor need a great writer's style set him strangely apart from his fellows; he does not *have* to take his material and 'make it strange'. Frank Kermode (in the big *Oxford Anthology of English Literature*, I. 504) reminds us that often something which we admire in a great author is 'merely a phrase, a turn, a strategy, an element of style, which he shares with even his tedious contemporaries, and that what we have admired is simply what defines our distance from his historical period'. This is an admirable argument for the close historical study of the language, as ancillary to the study of the literature. Unless we undertake this study of even so tangible a poet as Chaucer, we shall make sheer nonsense out of him, and our reading will be puerile; unless we apply it to Shakespeare, we shall neither (a) understand nor (b) assess the achievement of even so 'easy' a passage as Cassius's outburst on Julius Caesar:

> Ye gods, it doth amaze me,
> A man of such a feeble temper should
> So get the start of the majestic world,
> And bear the palm alone.

In school, I remember, we were taught of this passage only that *temper* meant 'temperament'; otherwise, apparently, it was within our grasp. But is *Ye gods* solemn (Rome being polytheistic at the time) or jocose, as in the easy-going *Ye gods and little fishes*? Is the vocative *Ye* very special (it would sound churchy to *us*), or is it as carelessly thrown in as is Shakespeare's 'mistaken' accusative in *Henry VIII*, 'Vain pomp and glory of this world, I hate ye'? Why does not Cassius say *does amaze* or *amazeth* or *amazes* (since all were available)?—has the periphrastic *doth* an extra note of solemnity and asseveration, or is it just a syllable-filler? Does *amaze* around 1600 convey a feeling of being in a labyrinth, or just of curious surprise? Was it slovenly in those days to omit the conjunction *that* before *A man*, or colloquial, or correct?—Chaucer often omitted it. Is *feeble* no more than we understand by it, or is it touched by *febrile*, 'feverish', too?—for Caesar had the falling sickness. Has *should* its sense of moral obligation? Is the strong enjambement, cutting the auxiliary off from *get*, the more exciting or modish for being unusual and contrived, or the less effective for being usual? How hackneyed (if at all) is the sustained athletic metaphor of starts and victors' palms? I am not proposing to answer these questions; but the responsible reader must ask them and find the answers, which will by the only path bring him to a real reading and appreciation.

If I am making the English of great writers sound too ordinary, too normal, too derived, too standard, I offer no apology; emulation of some past author, and acquiescence in the speech habits of our best contemporaries, are proper processes, and perhaps the startling new metaphor blasts prose with excess of light. Even in poetry, the Hungarian 'semantic' poet Stefan Themerson has been producing verse gutted of all the subjective nonsense, the irrelevant overtones, the atavistic memories, the figures, the analogues, and the nuances, and reducing each word to its dictionary definition; perhaps it sounds more enchanting in Magyar. But even if it is better for a prose-writer to ration himself over figures of speech, he must put his well chosen words in the best order; sometimes, for emotive or other effect, it may not be the usual speech-order, and earlier writers may therefore be too consequential for our taste. In verse, with Chaucer and for a long time after him, the usual sense-order was enough; it was only after centuries that an apothegm like

> Although we miss what we should choose,
> The greater happiness ensues.

could vary its precise conformity into the more charming, piquant, unbuttoned, off-rhymed chiasmus of

> Although what we should choose we miss,
> Ensues the greater happiness.

But this kind of flicker of new life is not a prose requirement, whereas the wonderfully apt word *is*.

Once the *mot juste* has been established, it may prove to be the only word for its detailed purpose; in such a case, elegant variation turns out to be inelegant indeed. We are studying a description of some embroidery:

In the lowest panel, four peacocks stand side by side with their tails displayed, their beaks pointing alternately to right and left; in the next cartouche, the same number are also shown in their pride, with the same alternation-motif though with the directions reversed; the topmost oval exhibits a similar arrangement to the bottom, and the same zigzagging effect...

This is neither bad, nor long enough to be tedious, but its wrigglings are fussy and unnecessary; the plan which it is setting out for us could be best expressed by a table with numbers and Ls and Rs, and the attempt to make it into varied and supple prose is wasted.

The right word for the earnest author may be a very wrong one for the normal reader. Perhaps the risk is greater in a compelling jet of subjective poetry, and I once read in a cosy magazine this idyllic programme of married love:

> On some unmisted hillside,
>   Where the light of the stars is strong,
> We'll share our thatch with the swallows,
>   And sing a common song.

This is so nice that it seems flippant and intruding to mis-interpret it; but the picture of his and her living over the rafters prepares us for the uproarious 'Ta-ra-ra-*boom*-de-ay!' or however it was that they were going to make the night hideous. And a vocabulary where every word is chosen, and matching, and stylistically linked, must be maintained to the end of its great polished sequences; no one would let old Macaulay down with a bump by setting off in his style (that style you couldn't tell the truth in, as Arnold held) and not luxuriating in it to the close: 'As feckless by disposition as he was ill-starred by heredity, the tenebrous circumstances of his diurnal existence combined with the graceless qualities of an impoverished intellect to produce in him an insatiable melancholy out of which he found it well-nigh impossible to snap'.

I hope that I have made it clear that I would give

recognition and praise to a common type of prose, not finding it mean or trite, and not circumscribing it so long as it served mind and ear well. I do not accord the same privileges to the common style of poetry, which arose quite a hundred years ago (I am not blaming the 1870 Education Act for it), and which has ranged from Newdigate Prize poems and Ella Wheeler Wilcox at one end down to cracker mottoes and Wilhelmina Stitch at the other. Verse has proved so easy to compose, and naturals can string together rhymes and rhythms so passably, that a handicap has been added—inversion: it isn't poetry, we seem to argue, unless it ties its syntax in little easy knots, and *then* it won't look like prose. Very strangely, although the motive is base the method gains some support from a study of any passage of verse which is composed in a prose-ordered syntax: however devoid of wit or invention, it becomes immediately amusing! When Belloc writes

> When George's grandmama was told
> That George had been as good as gold,
> She promised in the afternoon
> To buy him an immense balloon,

try substituting for *told* and *afternoon* the misrhymes and mismetres *informed* and *morning*, and you will feel no tingle of pleasure or jest. Straight syntax in narrative verse, it appears, confers sprightliness; but disordered syntax certainly doesn't ensure poetry. In school we sang to a fine old Welsh tune a botched English translation that started

> 'Without thy sire hast thou returned?'
> In grief the princess cried.

'Go back, or from my sight be spurned,
  To battle by his side.
I gave thee birth, but dashed [perhaps it was
    crashed; anyway, it wasn't *smashed*] to earth
  I'd sooner see thee lie
Or on thy bier [a perilous word with the young
    around] come carried here
  Than thus a craven die' [repeat the last two lines].

In the first line, the only possible prose order turns into
4.5.6.1.2.3; then 4.5.1.2.3; then 1.2.9.10.11.12.13.3.7.8.
4.5.6; and hops on with similar knight's moves. What is
achieved by this kind of technique?—showing no height-
ened vocabulary, no telling order, nothing strange that is
of any interest whatever, it merely makes verse odd and
hateful. Even the blankest of blank verse, by any poetaster
floundering in Milton's wake, is more reasonable than
this; we may scorn his lines as 'prose chopped up', but they
are likely to have at least the intelligibility of prose. And
the suave, convinced heroic couplets of the 'natural', who
has the Muse of pleasant tunes on his side even though the
Muse of deep meaning be aloof, go on demonstrating
down the ages the prose virtues of neatness, order, and
unblinding light.

It would seem that true poetry has little to say that will
help us to write true prose. To look at it in its coarsest
terms, its frequent structural members, rhyme and alliteration, are now held not to belong to prose; even a pure
rhyme occurring in prose is called a jingle, and I know
how frequent can be the ugly (and ambiguous, for which
modifies which?) strings of adverbs in -*ly*. I quote from a
recent PhD dissertation: 'The design was probably ori-

ginally totally symmetrical'. I believe that noises like this are with us because reading aloud is no longer a practised family and private art; writers are no longer hearing aloud, and the mind's ear is dulled. As for alliteration, it was before the Reformation the fibre of some of our best prose, and continued as a legitimate adornment; now it is winced at. The early-fourteenth-century mystic Richard Rolle, whose Latin is a brainstorm of alliteration, uses the figure with much more reserve in his English prose, until the pulse and excitement of it make him soar, or lapse, into a rough metre which is over-alliterated and big with earnestness. An anonymous earlier writer lets the martyred Juliana, one of the fearful saints in a sense not covered by the hymn, sneer at her tormentors with 'Beat as ye may beat, ye beadles of Belial!'; and throughout this little prose biography we get the impression of a thumping great girl who gave as good as she got, echoically. Later, to my regret, this admittedly easy figure was set aside; even in poetry it had its detractors as early as Chaucer's Parson, who didn't care for the 'rum, ram, ruf, by letter' technique—but, then, he had no preference for rhyme, either. A clearer voice, stating an aesthetic objection, is Sidney's in *Astrophel and Stella* (xv. 5–6):

> You that do dictionary's method bring
> Into your rhymes, running in rattling rows.

Even the pleasing cadences of poetry are now to be avoided in the writing of formal prose; they easily enter our speech, and I knew an enlightened family who always said *snap!* or *Basingstoke!* whenever a member used a sentence which was a blank verse line. It would be hard to

144

say whether a phrase like 'Rennie's conoidal triple-bladed screw' belongs to prose or verse; and I recall my relief and misgivings when the official wording 'Patroness of the Bristol Old Vic Trust' *just* fitted into the light-hearted couplets which I had the honour of writing to welcome HRH Princess Marina, Duchess of Kent, on one of her last public engagements.

Let prose be prose, then. However penetrating and apocalyptic a writer is, his prose will still not be satisfactory if, without effectiveness, it is unpunctuated, unparagraphed, riotous, sticky, serpentine, or downright queer; there are few—but a few—safe hands in which prose of these varieties can be formed to its abundant life. Some critics, however, anxious to be seen as recognising the onset of the new, condemn the old, in its grace, politeness, clarity, and traditionalism, as 'bellettristic', hateful word. I really believe that they are confused between the style of a standard writer and his inability or unwillingness to 'engage with' their critical, political, sociological, humanist, and especially sexual, concerns. So a small work, however well written, which is not revolutionary or 'concerned' or disturbing, is just 'belles lettres'. David Garnett's short novels I have heard classified thus, the beauty of their style being dismissed as irrelevant; whereas D. H. Lawrence's *St Mawr*, which in its inert conversations, its proposal of marriage, and its social gaffes, so often resembles *The Young Visiters*, is just bound to be great prose. Such criticism is certainly confused and perhaps dishonest. I do not wish to read *Reader's Digest*; its subjects would rarely interest me, I have time for formal reading of classics instead, and the butterfly approach of *any* popular magazine is not to my specialist tastes. But I do not make fun of its *style*, which is clear, adequate, and sort-of friendly; 'Perhaps so', says the literary critic, 'but its political alignments are conservative', and if he was reading its vivid account of a surgical operation or a tanker disaster, when a visitor called he would tuck it under the cushion as if it were some piece of childish depravity.

14

THE EVEN MORE DELICATE
SUBJECT OF TASTE

I have been defending belles-lettres; but, of course, praise
of them must sometimes be limited by their limited scope,
which includes trivialities. It is noticeable that the outwardly unworried and unhurried E. V. Lucas, always an
agreeable stylist, wrote little books with such titles as
Saunterer's Rewards, the gleanings of a nimble mind not one
bit obsessed with the wrath to come. We are sterner now;
the writer underplays his talent at his peril, and Paul
Dehn might argue that, while the Bomb exists, the only
allowable idiom of wit or poetry is that of his *Leaden
Treasury*, the idiom cowering under the grey and poisonous
wall. The subjects treated should be a matter of even
greater responsibility, yet what do we find, from the
meanest newspaper to the plushiest book? We may under-
standably get the impression that public censorship and
private discrimination, sacral religion and private devo-
tion, are alike unable or unwilling to prevent the spread of
depraving and corrupting reading-matter. Ian Robinson,
in *The Survival of English* (1973), speaks with gravity and a
proper venom of what he sees as pornography, pointing
out that it doesn't just *cause* depravity and corruption but

is depravity and corruption, and—closer to our present purpose—depraves and corrupts the common language. Certainly, a language where 'everything goes', where the foul, callous, sick, mindless, un-grown-up remark finds an accepted place, is as doomed as Nero. Mr Robinson quite rightly lets the pornography of lust and perversion be sinful in itself, and not just for the social damage it may do; but in this he may be underestimating the extent of that damage.

I do not know how far the station bookstall can be said to produce anything but a palliative for a long journey, the equivalent of the juvenile comic, crisps, and sheriff's toy hat. Only two main tastes are appeased, and that for the smoking gun is pretty harmless, since there can be little opportunity for precise emulation, though boots, flick-knives, and bicycle-chains capture the spirit of the thing. The other taste, that of the voyeur, timidest of all sexual perverts, is indulged by these gaudy booklets hollowly and disappointingly, the cover being the wildest bit, and the frustrated reader finding it all to be what James Thomson II calls 'confirmation of the old despair'. But bookshops where 'specialist tastes' are catered for, and where police action has been inhibited by fond lawgivers, are surely doing damage to the reader and so to those whom he influences; again, men who like books on Japanese prison camps or the rack will not normally be able to use them as manuals, but a few years ago we would have said the same about books on witchcraft, necromancy, black magic, grave-robbing, and other pretences to occult power, and now these practices are with us and are withering the brains and bodies of those whom they touch. Yet it is not the subject-matter of pornography that

148

misleads and upsets people of drifting direction and precarious balance, so much as the persuasive strength of its rhetoric; in a society sensible enough to recognise the existence of promiscuity, the habit can be mentioned and considered and unequivocally published, even with tenderness or laughter, but the pornographer's programme is callous and austere. I doubt whether any saucy limerick or fantastic anecdote ever moved a normal man to imagine mischief on his couch to another's disaster; but there is a phrasing in newspaper reports, and certainly in the leisured strategy of our franker novels, that must have fired many a turbulent spirit to go out and commit rape. Mr Robinson particularly mentions *Radcliffe* as a novel which would not necessarily corrupt, but 'might'; it seems to me bound to do so. It is the only positively dirty and depraved book on my shelves; analogy conned me into buying it, because the same author's *This Sporting Life* had been so wise, so realistic, and so compassionate. Admittedly, *Radcliffe* would make an awkward blueprint for vice, because the equipment needed includes a motor-bike, a private altar, an unusual sandwich-filling, a comedian with a psychosomatic limp, a fey sister, sinister uncles, reams and reams of drawing-paper, and enormous hammers; also, whereas I understand English domestic architecture better than Mr Storey does, and the symbolism of black dogs that cross one's path, the symbolism of marquee-pegs is closed to me. But what can a book like this achieve, save to dismay and disturb?—and all to no constructive purpose whatever; one of the sunlit scenes is a field awash with sewage, which is overt enough as a symbol.

Radcliffe, novel of its year in the critics' eyes, is of course not just illiterate filth, though I think it is over-written, especially in its repeated trick of the adverb phrase that has to hedge so many of the doings and sayings of all the devious and unrealised characters: 'with a kind of minute vexation', 'with a stiffened gesture, almost a caricature of obeisance', and so on, as if to ascribe motives where no clear motive would cover the astonishing deed or word. My first experience of that other proven masterpiece, now snugly called *Lady C*, was of sitting in a stationary train at Bath Spa (of all stations) while three youths stamped along the corridor opening the doors and shouting the released word; a new age had dawned, and no element of the language could ever again be condemned as wayward. How *right* it was made to seem, that no subject should be unmentionable! Every topic is the better for an airing, and as a further snub to those who still wanted to keep one topic in a fine and private place it was pointed out that greater obscenities had not only been getting by in print, but had been on the school curriculum: so there was derisory mention of the obscenity of war, of patriotism, of fox-hunting, of class-distinction, of racism, each of which had their pornography of resonant verse, or ponderous treatise, or handsome sporting-print. Now it is easy and sensible to find much, or almost everything, that is ab-horrent in war and hunting and social injustice, but it is a misuse of the lexicon to apply the words *obscenity* and *pornography* to these subjects and their publication, or to pretend that links such as a stepfather's cruelty or the Mars-and-Venus theme prove the whole documentation of humanity to be one vast pornography of which sex is the most allowable element, not the least. Books in the most lavish praise of Wellington, William Tell, John Peel, Lord Curzon, or even Hitler, will not have even slightly the same effect of warping and unhingeing the doors of the mind as will exposure, in the trying years between three and eighteen, and beyond, to the grand plea for lasciviousness.

Cruel frankness, with a sluggish vein of sex, reached new deeps in 1974 when the gifted Kingsley Amis produced *Getting On*. This is not a useful true record of the aged in community; it is deliberate fiction, and stranger than necessary in that the broken creatures that inhabit it are only in their 70s, not such a glum age in present-day society. Why did he write it?—to show how he could observe tired malice with malice, pitifulness with pitilessness, bowel and kidney disorganisation with a snigger, and the long death of hope with an exultant whoop? It has been rightly called witty and outrageous; in it, taste and decency (that which is *decens*, 'fitting') are finally reduced by a clever, clever process. Mr Amis has occasioned the sin of others, in that they have cursed him with 'He'll be old himself one day', a natural but unchristian reaction; I think that he should receive Berowne's sentence, 'To move wild laughter in the throat of death', by serving for a year in a geriatric ward.

And let those who feel that full publication of any sexual theme is the ultimate in release, and fulfilment, and joy, reflect that it was said not long ago, of a certain country: 'In no country in the world is sex thought about, talked about, and written about, so much—and enjoyed so little'.

When all else that was once treated with respect and reserve is exposed to lurid candour and challenge, it is not surprising that religion has been subjected to humiliation; not to a Christian invitation that it should humble itself, but to a coarsening and degradation in print and to blasphemy in speech. Obscene expletives, the violent physical language of the field of battle or the rugby field, have always had their apologists, and man's built-in sexuality is a sufficient explanation; but man's built-in spirituality is real, too, and its sudden expression is in urgent prayer, not in blasphemy. It is disappointing to hear highly educated people, academics in plenty and atheists as well, whose surprise or emphasis is normally conveyed by the Word *Christ*. In principle, they could argue, this is no 'worse' than using the disguised *Goodness!* or *Gee!*, though the honest among them would admit that no educated person needs expletives or uses them as anything but gap-fillers, the arthritis at the joints of speech. So it is odd for gifted persons to discourse so inexpressively, the great Word being dead and unmeant to them; and the considerate might also reflect that they would not enjoy the moment when the name of their loved father or mother, no longer in this world, was lightly used by someone else in offhand asseveration or for no reason at all—and this is the measure of the offence that *they* give to Christians by their blasphemy. My request is a moderate one here, that the gift of speech be used for efficient and civilised conversation, not for wasteful rudeness. It is not enough that a common language should exist in which various disciplines can be shared and many ideas aired for discussion; Mother Julian of Norwich long ago warned us against taking familiarity so far as to forget courtesy, and when the blasphemer wounded the believer with a word, the medieval mind saw it as another wound on the crucified body of Christ. We may now view it only as discourteous folly; but mindless it certainly is, a variation of the pure Mellors spoken by louts at a Glasgow football match.

Even when I use a loaded word such as *civilised*, and the hecklers crowd in and ask what I mean by civilisation, afternoon tea at Grantown-on-Spey or soup for the dying in Calcutta, 'the doubter and the doubt' still belong to the human family and its common language, and our approach to one another needs this real sense of brotherhood; we must not obstruct by insult, or deliberately cut our means of communication. I am assuming that we do not wish to be reduced to talking in shrieks or grunts, and that we wish to go on communicating. When Professor Frank George said in the Unilever magazine in 1969 that 'the potential of the computer in the world of thought is perhaps as great, if not greater, than that of the human being', he meant, of course, 'as great as, if not greater than, that of the human being', but his incoherent grammar chokes me less than does the awful threat.

I began this book with the present and the familiar; during the course of it, I have had to work back to the past and studied, but my deep concern is with the present state of a very great language possessed of a very great literature. It is not yet at risk, though some of its practitioners are treating it hysterically, or sullenly, or insolently; we cannot yet hear in it the mourning hum as of the bees in a dying hive, and its wide spread and its easy efficacy seem bound to ensure it a lasting life in *some* form. But the form matters desperately: it matters that the language should be clear, melodious, interesting, regionally varied but not socially or morally debased, dependent on the best of the past, adaptable to the promise of the future, a key to the wisdom of the years, and an ordered system that imposes order on our living.

INDEX

Germanic languages, 15, 27, 30, 74
Gloucestershire dialect, 67
Gnomes in advertising, 117–18
God, 52, 102, 152
Gowers, Sir Ernest, 88–9, 94, 101, 105, 126
Graffiti, 131
Grammatical inflexions, 9–11, 14, 17, 21, 34, 38, 43–50, 52, 83–4, 120
Greek, 9, 15, 30, 40, 47, 75–7, 79, 101

Headlines, 46, 57, 86–7
Heralds' English, 107–8
Heroic couplets, 143
Hiss, ubiquitous, 35–40
Hopefully, improper, 95
Humour, 46–7
Hymns, 24–5
Hyperbole in advertising, 114

Icelandic, 27
Idiolects, 68
If, improper, 90–1
If he'd've known, 55
Imperative, 60–1
Inanimates can't 'possess', 38–9
Indefinite article, 47
Individual = person, 128
-ing, 10, 38–9, 48
Initial Teaching Alphabet, 77–8
Innuendo in advertising, 114

Interrogative, 61, 80
Inversion in poetry, 11, 142–3
Italian, 73

Jargon, 106–35
Journalese, 90, 95, 109–12

Lancashire dialect, 77
Latin, 15, 17–18, 21, 29, 47, 58–9, 72–3, 90, 99, 101, 130, 144
Lawyers' English, 106–7
Letter-writing, 42, 127
Limerick, 149
Limitation of meaning, 18–22
'Linguistics' English, 135
Literally, improper, 22, 93
Liturgies, 24–5, 51
Liverpuddlian, 66, 123
London, 63–5, 68, 73
Lying in advertising, 115–16

-manship, 44
Meaning, 8–10, 18–24
'Media', 121–4, 127–8, 130
Medical and scientific English, 108–9
Memorial doggerel, 111–12
Mercian, 63
Metaphor, 13, 99, 137–9
Middle English, 19, 21–2, 52, 64, 103
Monosyllables, 10, 12, 40–1
Mot juste, 140–1
Musicologists' English, 132
mutated plurals, 49–50

157